ENDORSEMENTS

"As the pastor of a church that's located right next to a major university, I know how challenging college can be for the faith of many students. Austin has written a helpful resource that will help you face the challenges you face with college, rooted in the gospel. I recommend every college student and potential college student to read this little book."
- Matt Carter, The Austin Stone Community Church, *Austin, TX*

"Austin writes with clever analogy and wise practicality. Easy to read and packed with helpful tips on doing college life well rather than being used towards the dangers of skepticism, apathy, or moralism. As a minister on college campuses around the world for nearly 25 years, I would recommend this read to students wholeheartedly."
- Miles O'Neill, Cru Campus Director, UNC Chapel Hill, *Chapel Hill, NC*

"Entering a new chapter of life such as college can be one of the most difficult times if you aren't equipped. This book will certainly equip and empower you to live a life on mission for His glory, and challenge you to remain rooted in your identity in Christ amidst a world that tells you otherwise. As a former youth pastor and now lead pastor of a large church with many millennials, I highly recommend it."
- Joby Martin, Lead Pastor, The Church of Eleven22, *Jacksonville, FL*

"I have known Austin all his life, and have watched God grow, stretch, season and mature him into an incredibly insightful young minister. 10 *Things Every Christian Should Know For College* is one of the most useful and unique books I have read in a long time. Austin's desire is to help prepare, equip, and empower students for what they will face in today's university setting. This will soon be on every parent's list and in every student's book bag."

- Dr. Mac Brunson, Lead Pastor, First Baptist Jacksonville, *Jacksonville, FL*

"Leaving home and heading to college is something too many high school graduates are ill prepared to face. Place this little book in their hands and give them a 'head start' for the exciting and challenging journey that is ahead of them."

- Daniel L. Akin, PhD., *President of Southeastern Baptist Theological Seminary*

"Christian young people getting ready to enter college are often worried about what the college experience will do to their faith. They have heard how many young people walk away from their faith during their college years while others are harassed for trying to stand up for their faith. Austin has faced the challenge of staying true to his faith while in college, and not only survived but thrived in the experience. He shares what to expect and how to practically keep your walk with the Lord strong while at college. 10 *Things Every Christian Should Know For College* is a must read for every Christian entering college for the first time."

- Glen Schultz, Ed.D., Director of Kingdom Education Ministries Author: *Kingdom Education: God's Plan for Educating Future Generations*

"Austin hits the bullseye in 10 *Things Every Christian Should Know For College*. Fresh out of university himself, he provides a reasoned and practical approach to walking closely with Christ during this critically important season of life. This book could be key in preventing college students from 'throwing away' their faith or 'putting it on the shelf' during their days on campus. Instead, students are encouraged to embrace the unique opportunities provided in college life, and to enjoy the process of impacting the culture through a winsome and thoughtful daily approach."

- Richard Hardee, Head of School, Calvary Baptist Day School, *Winston-Salem, NC*

"We are proud to have Austin as a graduate of High Point Christian Academy. He successfully transitioned from our small Christian high school to a large secular university where he continued to grow in his faith by applying the principles he describes in this book. His ten recommendations for young people going to college are very practical but ingenious. This book will be an excellent guide for any Christian student venturing off to college who wants to continue growing in faith. I highly recommend this book!"

- Keith Curlee, Head of School, High Point Christian Academy, *High Point, NC*

"Austin has provided a resource that I wish was around my freshman year of college. This will give a student a gospel-centered confidence that encourages the freedom to learn, to question and to engage without the fear of losing their faith. I will make sure this book is in the hands of every graduating high school senior in our church."

- Rob Pacienza, Lead Pastor of Coral Ridge Presbyterian Church, *Fort Lauderdale, FL*

10 THINGS EVERY CHRISTIAN SHOULD KNOW FOR COLLEGE

A STUDENT'S GUIDE ON DOUBT, COMMUNITY, & IDENTITY

AUSTIN GENTRY

10 Things Every Christian Should Know For College: A
Student's Guide on Doubt, Community, & Identity

© 2018 by Austin Gentry
All rights reserved.

ISBN 978-0692050958

Gentry Publishing

Printed in the United States of America

To High Point Christian Academy
May you continue to be a hub that disciples students,
preparing them to be ambassadors for Christ on the college campus

A WORD OF THANKS

To God, thank you for your amazing grace in my life. Thank you for constantly leading me and guiding me—for bringing me to the university I never thought I'd attend, but to the university you knew I needed to attend for four years of my life. Thank you for allowing me the opportunity to write this book and for empowering me to do so. My life has been nothing short of your amazing grace in every way.

To Mom and Dad, I am so appreciative of you. You two are the best. There are thousands of ways I could thank you. Just know that I wouldn't have been able to write this book without you. Your constant support, encouragement, and love have been the most tangible displays of God's character to me over the course of my life.

To Jonathan Edwards and Chris Pappalardo, for your talent and wisdom in the editing process. I couldn't have been more fortunate to have you two as my editors. This book would not nearly be as clear, helpful, and impactful without you.

To Nick Nohling, Miles O'Neill, and J.D. Greear, for being the most formative, pastoral influences in my life throughout college. I don't know who I would be without your leadership. Your discipling, teaching, and preaching have shaped me profoundly.

Finally, to my many friends and acquaintances in college, you've been a huge inspiration to me. My shared experiences with you—be it in the dorm, cafeteria, or classroom—have been the grounds for this book. I stand in grateful debt to every one of you in more ways than one.

"Against the world; for the world."

—St. Athanasius

CONTENTS

FOREWORD

I remember my first night in college, lying on my bed thinking, "I could get up and go anywhere I want right now, with anyone. I would not have to ask anyone's permission, and no one would even ask where I was. I am literally *free*." It felt liberating. And terrifying.

My high school youth pastor always said, "You can't really give your life to Christ until it's yours to give." College is the first time when, for many, your life is truly 'yours.' During these four years, you will set priorities, forge relationships, and make decisions that shape the rest of your life. Choose wisely, and you'll reap rich rewards.

I wish I had had a book like Austin's during those days. It would have prepared me for the unique challenges college was about to present to my spiritual life. In these pages, Austin unpacks 10 of the most important issues students must grapple with as they navigate their college experience. How you respond to these challenges will determine not only your success in college, but in your life, and in some cases, your eternity.

I've had the privilege of knowing and working with Austin for quite some time. He is creative, insightful, and authentic. There's not a pretentious bone in his body, and he lives what he writes. His transparency will sometimes startle but always encourage you. As you're engrossed in the story of his journey, you'll find wisdom for your own. This book is fresh, reflective, and practical. And just downright enjoyable to read.

Right before I left for college my dad shared Matthew 6:33 with me, a verse that was to become one of my life verses: "Seek first the Kingdom of God and his righteousness, and all these things will be added to you."

Reading 10 *Things Every Christian Should Know For College*, and implementing its principles, is a great way of applying that verse. I commend this book to you enthusiastically.

J.D. Greear, Ph.D.
Lead Pastor, the Summit Church, *Raleigh*, NC

ALARM CLOCKS, SKYDIVING, EMINEM, AND A NEW MENTAL TOOLBOX

I jolted awake, except this time without an alarm clock.

And I can't do anything without an alarm clock.

I was shaking a little. Sweating a little.

My heart was thumping. My mind was racing. My hands were twitching.

It wasn't fear. It wasn't elation.

It was *the day*.

The day I would leave for college.

My sleep cycle must have been synced up with that all-too-familiar count-down calendar I observed every morning on our refrigerator, reminding me that I was one day closer to that monumental, mid-August day—the day that was circled 3 times in red, marked 7 times with notes, and starred 4 times just for added excitement—*and that day was today*.

The time had finally come.

And now it was finally time to go.

Every nerve in my body shook with adrenaline. I felt like I had been wired to a power plant of nervous energy, and its electricity surged through me like a natural conduit.

Excitement. Apprehension.
Thrill. Angst.
The anticipation of pursuing the new and unknown.
The anxiety of leaving behind the familiar and known.

Imagine the exhilaration of skydiving. Suiting up, strapping in, and taking off—all doing so with the invigorating thought in the front of your mind, *"Wow! I'm actually about to do this!"* Then walking hesitantly up to the edge of the plane's doorway and falling rapidly into the vast, blue expanse with nothing but a parachute to catch you.

In a similar way, the college experience can feel a lot like that, too. The feelings you get before stepping onto campus for the first time can be somewhat similar to the feelings you get before stepping off a plane and skydiving for the first time. You are launching into a new altitude of life, jumping out of your comfort zone, and diving headfirst into the vast unknown with only the parachute of your own past experiences to catch you. And once you take that step of faith, you'll be flying through a new atmosphere of unknowns at a break-neck speed. You won't exactly feel 'settled' per se for quite some time, but that's simply part of the experience.

Personally, the feelings that electrified me that mid-August morning continued to buzz throughout the first couple months of school. The lyrics *Lose Yourself* played through the soundtrack of my tensed mind during that season, on repeat:

> *"Palms were sweaty, knees weak, arms were heavy...*
> *This opportunity comes once in a lifetime..."*

Now, Eminem wasn't exactly referring to the college experience in those lyrics, and he's certainly not a theologian I would endorse. However, his words nevertheless describe the overall sentiment quite well: opportunities that come once in a lifetime not only exhilarate us, but also require something of us.

And the opportunity of going to college is definitely one of them.

For those of you who have picked up this book and are currently in college, you can probably look back at the start of your first year and relate to those dynamic feelings all too well. You know that college can be a whirlwind in more ways than one. You're aware of its many challenges, unknowns, highs, and lows.

And for those of you who have picked up this book and are getting ready to take that first step into college, you don't know what to expect. You're currently in the waiting line, eagerly anticipating what those new challenges, unknowns, highs, and lows will be like once you get there.

Wherever you are along this journey, the college experience is truly unlike anything else. Everything is completely new. Everything is completely unknown.

For those reasons, it can be incredibly exciting. But for those same exact reasons, it can be rather nerve-racking as well, especially when it comes to your faith.

Whether you're a rising freshman or an upcoming senior, it's likely that you've already dealt with the thoughts of...

What if a professor challenges my beliefs?
What if I can't find Christian community?
What if I can't find a good church to go to?
What if I lose my way?

If you have wrestled with these questions, just know that you are in the large majority. These are extremely common questions and concerns in this new stage of life.

However, even though these kinds of questions are relatively common, that doesn't make them any less daunting or disconcerting, either. In fact, the reason they may seem so daunting is because they appear to threaten and shake the very pillars of who we are—our sense of reality, our sense of self, and our sense of belonging.

That can be rather unnerving. But there's only one thing that can be more unnerving than having your pillars shaken—and that's *not knowing how to respond when you are shaken.*

Truth is, no matter who you are, college will test you and shake you at some level.

It could be intellectual questions you won't initially know how to answer.

No matter who you are, college will test you and shake you at some level.

It could be ethical choices you won't initially know how to respond to.

It could be different narratives about sexuality, different perspectives about culture, and different viewpoints about religion that you won't initially know how to grapple with.

There's nothing wrong with encountering and even being challenged by these worldviews and lifestyles. In fact, in many ways, it's a good thing that you are exposed to them. But the question becomes, what do you do when it happens?

For example, when you hear a skeptical claim, how should you respond? Do you naively believe it or blindly reject it? How are you to do the balancing act of being intellectually curious and yet religiously grounded at the same time?

Or, when you encounter an ethical dilemma, how should you react? Do you quietly compromise your faith at the expense of being relatable, or do you boldly affirm your faith at the risk of being 'holier than thou'? How are you to do the balancing act of making the right decision and yet maintaining your friendships at the same time?

How are you to do the balancing act of being intellectually curious and yet religiously grounded at the same time?

Truly, the whole experience can be somewhat disorienting, especially if you're not expecting it. From academic challenges in the classroom to social dilemmas on the weekend, it'll happen to the best of us.

I can remember the first time a professor challenged my faith. And my gut reaction? Intellectual and spiritual paralysis. I wanted to remain steadfast in my Christian faith, but I didn't want to sacrifice being intellectually authentic, either. I can also remember the first time a friend encouraged me to go partying with him, where there would be underage drinking and immodest behavior. And my initial reaction? Paralysis once again. I wanted to be a Christian witness, but I didn't want to sacrifice our friendship by appearing 'better' than him, either.

How are you to do the balancing act of making the right decision and yet maintaining your friendships at the same time?

In both of those instances, I felt like an insect of prey, caught in the entangling webs of contrasting worldviews and alternative lifestyles. I knew what I believed, and I knew what I wanted to do, but I didn't have any practical solutions that would help me break free. I just didn't know what to think or how to respond. And so, I felt *stuck*.

Many Christian college students will encounter sticky situations like these as well—where the main issue is not the challenges, dilemmas, or 'webs' themselves, but rather, the issue of how to respond when confronted by them.

But why? Why is it such a challenge to know how to respond?

I think it's because the conceptual 'tools' we so often used to address the challenges of our *pre-college* days no longer works for the entirely different set of challenges we'll face for our *in-college* days. We get hit with the startling realization that our mental 'toolbox' has become rather unhelpful and obsolete for approaching this new, collegiate stage of life.

To be sure, you will encounter various questions, challenges, and unknowns, but rest in this: a true Christian is not someone whose faith is never shaken, but instead, someone who knows how to faithfully respond *when they are shaken*.

> *A true Christian is not someone whose faith is never shaken, but instead, someone who knows how to faithfully respond when they are shaken.*

So the question becomes, how should you respond? How should you prepare? How do you bridge the gap between claiming Christ in high school to following Christ in college? How do you effectively navigate through all the highs and lows that are inevitable parts of the college experience?

That's precisely why I wrote this small book. I want to help the average Christian feel prepared, equipped, and empowered to face the unique challenges of college.

This small book provides 10 practical pointers—or, some new

conceptual 'tools'—for how to best approach some of the most common questions and concerns related to the university experience. Pointers 1–5 focus on how to best prepare for the intellectual and theological challenges that will come your way, and Pointers 6–10 provide some practical advice that you can implement right away—whether you're currently in college or about to take that bold step into it.

The last thing I want is for any of you to go through college *passively* or *defensively* as a Christian. Rather, I want you to live *proactively* and *influentially* as a Christian. I don't want you to feel like you're always *on your heels*, pushing back against the force of new temptations and different worldviews. I want you feel like you're readily *on your toes*, confidently equipped for what to expect and how to respond.

To those of you who are about to embark upon the college campus, you're likely caught between that dynamic tension of both nervousness and excitement. Maybe you're excited for a new environment, but nervous about how you'll connect with others. Maybe you're excited to learn new subjects, but nervous about how you'll engage with skeptical professors. Leaving the safety of the homeland and exploring the unknowns of the uncharted will certainly have its challenges.

And to those of you who are currently navigating through the unique waters of college, it's possible that you could be anywhere on the horizon of enjoyment to disappointment, depending on your current situation. Yet, even on the best of days, there can still be some type of struggle. Maybe you're feeling intellectually adrift in the waves of skepticism; maybe your sails are failing to catch the delightful wind of community; maybe you're feeling shipwrecked upon the shores of isolation; maybe you're having a hard time hoisting the banner of your faith in the classroom; or maybe you're simply striving to gain a clearer sense of direction for what to do when certain obstacles come your way.

Whatever the case may be, it's my hope and prayer that this small book might inject a bold sense of confidence in you and impart a great sense of peace to you—wherever you are along this important journey.

Let's begin by discussing some of the main challenges that exist in the university environment.

You ready?

Let's do it.

PART 1

PROFESSORS, SKEPTICISM, DOUBT... AND THE MIND OF THE CHRISTIAN COLLEGE STUDENT

YOUR PROFESSOR IS SMART, BUT NOT OMNISCIENT

"But test everything; hold fast what is good."
-1 Thessalonians 5:21

Have you seen or heard of the popular Christian movie, *God's Not Dead*? The movie tells the story of a Christian college student, Josh Wheaton, who enters his freshman year of college and immediately finds himself struggling to keep the faith. The film opens with Josh arriving to campus and finding his way to his very first class, Philosophy 101. He discovers, however, that this class happens to be taught by one of the university's most vocal atheists, Dr. Radisson, who's notorious for seeking to destroy the religious faith of his students. The plotline essentially involves Josh's intense struggle with Dr. Radisson—one depicted by a slew of personal doubts, tireless study sessions, and epic showdowns in the classroom. The movie ultimately aims to portray the tense dynamic at play in the modern day, university classroom: a Christian student struggling against an atheistic professor.

Now, if someone asked you the question, "What are you most fearful of in the university environment as a Christian?", there's a good chance the *first thing* that came to your mind was the daunting thought of the stereotypical, secular, university professor.

Based on all the horror stories out there about Christians forsaking their faith once they get to college, it can be easy to point the finger at university professors as the main cause. *They hate Christianity! They teach lies! They promote their own agenda!*

One could even make the argument that Christians tend to view such professors in a way not too dissimilar from the 'dementor' figure described in J. K. Rowling's wizarding world of *Harry Potter*. If you're unfamiliar with the narrative, dementors are looming, terrifying creatures that not only guard the infamous prison of Azkaban, but also haunt the campus grounds of Hogwarts. They're dangerous precisely because they can literally suck the souls out of their victims, leaving them utterly lifeless.

In a similar way, Christians can view secular professors in a comparatively dark light, seeing them as 'academic dementors' who haunt the 'Hogwarts' of the college institution, desperately seeking to extract every ounce of religious vitality from our hearts and minds. It's easy to think they connive in teaching against us, thrive in yielding more power than us, and strive in 'sucking' the faith out of us. And we...? Well, we just try to survive.

And so, the stereotype of the average, university professor can be one that is marked by staunchly anti-Christian, antagonistic, and belittling sentiments. We can hastily label them as dooming figures who will *personally* challenge our faith, *personally* embarrass us in front of class, and *personally* fail us if we do not submit to their point of view.

But is that a fair or accurate view of these professors?

'Who' You Can Expect

Generally, Christians shouldn't expect that type of hostile experience. To be fair to the majority of university professors, these stereotypes and assumptions are, in fact, gross exaggerations and embellishments. While the movie, *God's Not Dead*, does portray an important dynamic between the Christian student and the university professor, it does embellish the level of hostility in the average classroom environment. Very few secular professors approach their classroom setting as a 'Roman Coliseum' of sorts where they set their teeth on destroying the faith of their Christian students.

It's important to note that by law, all public university professors are required to teach from a secular perspective (i.e., the assumption that God does not exist). However, you might get some comfort in how that actually plays out in the classroom. In reality...

- A large majority of professors will teach from a secular perspective, and in so doing, they will teach *passively* against Christianity.
- A small minority of professors will not only teach from a secular perspective, but they will also take it a step further and teach *actively* against Christianity.
- But only a slight percentage of professors will go so far as to attack you *personally* as a Christian.

While there is usually a surplus of non-Christian professors and a scarcity of Christian professors, it is highly unlikely that you will be *personally* attacked for your faith. (I'm not saying that it won't happen for certain, but I am saying there's a good chance it won't happen in general.)

So, be at rest. This means you can take the needle of objectivity and pop some of those over-inflated stereotypes of secular professors, and in so doing, dissipate some of insubstantial fear that's so often associated with them.

At the same time, however, I don't want you to be overly optimistic, either, and fail to see a clear university agenda standing in direct contrast to the biblical worldview. That leads me to 'what' you can expect to hear. So whether your professors teach passively or actively against Christianity, here are some things you can expect to hear from them insofar as claims, approaches, and content is concerned.

'What' You Can Expect

Overall, there are two common themes/tactics you need to be aware of.

First, you can expect your professor to make claims that he knows will rock the boat of conventional Christian belief. This can happen in virtually any class you are in: Biology, Sociology, Political Science, English, Philosophy, or Religion.

For example, you might hear...

"Evolution is a theory, just like gravity is a theory."
"Christianity is responsible for the slave trade."
"Can God create a rock heavier than He can lift?"

When I first heard these types of claims, I didn't know how to process. I started to think, *"Had the church been lying to me all my life? This professor has a PhD at the end of his name... so his statements must be correct, right?"*

It's not unusual to think the same thing when that happens to you, too. It's possible for these types of claims to rattle you quite a bit because you might not have heard them before. So let's take a brief look at them since they're likely to come up eventually.

Biology/Evolution

* Evolution will certainly find its way into academic conversations, whether it's stated directly or assumed indirectly. The problem comes when professors and/or other students make bigger assertions about evolution than science actually warrants. For example, you might hear people say that evolution is a 'theory' just like gravity or the atom. The line of logic goes, *"If gravity and atoms are considered 'theories'—but are obviously true—then we should assume the theory of evolution is just as true, too! Basic logic!"* But that's being too hasty, and for one very important reason.

    You can expect your professor to make claims that he knows will rock the boat of conventional Christian belief.

    When we think of evolution in general, we tend to imagine a fish that became a bird, which became an ape, which became a human. But that type of evolution is *not* a theory like gravity or the atom. The only type of evolution that *is* a theory like gravity or the atom is *microevolution*, which theorizes that small, genetic adaptations take place in a species over time to help them better survive in a certain environment.

Macroevolution, however, assumes that large genetic changes can take place over time (like a fish becoming a bird, or an ape becoming a human). But this is *not* a theory like gravity or the atom because it's not testable or proven by science. Macroevolution is simply a conjecture of extrapolating the theory of microevolution.[1]

> **Professors and/or students tend to make bigger assertions about evolution than science actually warrants.**

So, when someone says, "*Evolution is as certain as gravity*," or something of the sorts, realize they're making an unwarranted jump that glazes over a critical distinction between microevolution and macroevolution. When they say this, they're not only overstepping the boundaries of science, but they're also showcasing their bias in neon lights.

Sociology/Slavery

• Moreover, you might also hear that slavery and imperialism originated from 'Christianized Europe.' That's not untrue, for the slave trade did start there. Yet, professors may often take it a step further and accuse Christian convictions for *fueling* those atrocities. If anything, however, history proves just the opposite. It was actually Christians—being compelled by their Christian beliefs—who were responsible for leading the Abolitionist Movement, ending the slave trade once and for all.[2] The footprint of the slave trade and imperialism can make Christianity an easy target, but that doesn't make it the cause, either.

Philosophy/Theology

- Additionally, your professors might also try to trap you with sly philosophical questions. A famous one is, "Can God create a rock heavier than He can lift?" But the problem with these types of questions is that they're already spring-loaded with an inherent logical trap. As soon as you try to step forward and answer, you'll get ensnared no matter how you respond.

  How so? Take the question above, for example. If God is *able* to create a rock heavier than He can lift, that means his divinity is limited because He can't lift it. At the same time, however, if He's *not* able to create a rock heavier than He can lift, then that means his divinity is limited there, too, because He can't create it. Either way, the result is the same: a picture of a God who seemingly fails to be God.

  But questions like these essentially ask God to make a 'square-circle' or a 'married-bachelor.' They're logical impossibilities that are conceptually contradictory by nature—not limits on God himself. These types of arguments are neither sound nor honest because built into them is a desire to get a certain answer. They might seem intellectually astute on the surface, but they are conceptually hollow in content. They're designed simply to dishevel you more than anything else.

You will hear many things like these examples above. Some claims will certainly be more legitimate than others, but there's always more to what you might hear.

Here's what I want to reaffirm to you: *While your professor is academically competent, he is not academically omniscient.*

To be sure, your professor unquestionably knows more than you do...

about a lot of things. But don't let that scare you. In terms of some claims he might make, just know that he might be partly right. But, he might be partly wrong, too. And in some cases, he might be completely wrong. In fact, in other cases, it might not even be an issue of 'right or wrong' per se, just an issue of absurdity.

While your professor is academically competent, he is not academically omniscient.

And that leads to a second important theme you need to watch out for.

You can expect that your professor will, from time to time, emphasize an obscure interpretation of some evidence that actually doesn't hold any weight in the scholarly community anyways. In fact, he himself probably knows that, too. But he also knows that *you don't know that. And that's precisely why he can get away with it so easily.*

For example, you might hear...

"There are 2000 errors in the New Testament."
"There are two creation accounts in Genesis, and they contradict each other."
"The Israelites never crossed the Red Sea. They crossed the Reed Sea, which is 2 feet deep."

These types of claims can be rattling as well. Your professor might say them with an air of confidence, but that doesn't mean they're substantial. A good rule of thumb is that if something sounds really far-fetched... it probably is. Claims like these are usually more full of shock factor than they are full of truth.

- For instance, hearing about the 'thousands of errors' in the New

Testament for the first time can be quite disturbing. But what most professors don't clarify is what kind of criteria they're using to determine 'errors' anyways. Most of the things they count as 'errors' are simply nothing more than scribal slip-ups or different spellings of words. It would be similar to using the words 'color' (American English) and 'colour' (British English) interchangeably. It wouldn't change the meaning of the text at all. It's the same word; it's just spelled differently. But according to them, that qualifies as an 'error.'[3]

- Or, hearing that there are 'two creation accounts' in Genesis that contradict each other can be rather unsettling, too. You might think, "I've read the creation account so many times. How could I have skimmed over something that would seem so obvious?" Genesis 2 starts by summarizing what happened in Genesis 1, and some scholars interpret that summary to be a completely different creation account altogether. Some people think Genesis 1 is the poetic version and Genesis 2 is the prose version of the same story. People can fall on different spectrums and have different perspectives. But even if there are two types of creation accounts, it doesn't mean the entire creation account is false, fabricated, or contradictory, either. That, too, would be taking an unwarranted jump.[4]

> *You can expect your professor, from time to time, to emphasize an obscure interpretation of evidence that doesn't hold much weight in the scholarly community anyways.*

- And you might even hear that the Israelites crossed the *Reed Sea*, not the *Red Sea*. To the academic community, that seems more realistic since the Reed Sea is a shallow pond that can easily be crossed by foot, whereas the Red Sea is not. They might say, "It *was probably a mis-communication, carried down for the sake of legend!*" to explain away one of the most famous miracles in the Bible. However, what's funny is that they don't realize they're actually implying a miracle themselves in doing so: namely, suggesting that the entire Egyptian army drowned in 2-feet of water in the Reed Sea. To me, that sounds like almost as much of a miracle as the Israelites crossing the Red Sea on foot.

You can generally expect the academic community to dismiss any-thing that's supernatural in the Bible. Their reason is because science can't confirm it (even though *that's the point...* it's 'super' natural, above nature). And so, they'll retell supernatural events in a way that fits their non-supernatural view of the world. They'll either say the supernatural event didn't happen, or that it's simply a myth, even if the account wasn't written with the markings of mythology.

Unfortunately, when professors make shocking claims, it can lead students to immediately question everything. But when this happens, you need to know one very important truth: there is substantial scholarship elsewhere that can expose these claims to be nothing more than mere exaggerations, embellishments, or misinterpretations.

> *Your professor is certainly smart, but there are other scholars in his field of study who are just as smart as he is, who may fundamentally disagree with his conclusions.*

Your professor is certainly smart; however, there are other scholars in his same field of study who are likely just as smart as he is (Christian and non-Christian alike) and who may fundamentally disa-gree with his conclusions. In fact, they may even scoff at some of the things your professor might say in class.

Problem is, you usually won't hear other angles of legitimate scholarship in class because there's only one professor in the room. And this is especially true when the topic involves Christianity. You just won't hear legitimate scholarship against *secular claims*... from your *secular professors*... at a *secular university*... and understandably so. If there are any apparent 'evidences' or 'data' that can be used to compete against Christianity, you will likely hear those things instead.

But be assured that there is sufficient evidence for Christianity across the board that no secular scholarship has proven otherwise. Christianity has stood up under the most intense critiques and evaluations of secular scholarship for over 2000 years. It has proven the tests of time, and it will continue to prove the tests of time, too.

I highly recommend you buying two books that address the most common objections made against the Old and New Testament: A *Survey of Old Testament Introduction* by Gleason Archer and *Heresy of Orthodoxy* by Köstenberger and Kruger. And for more information on objections to the Bible, I would encourage you to check out the website, www.ehrmanproject.com. Here, you will find a host of short videos from the world's leading biblical scholars that address the most common objections to the Bible in a 2-5 minute format. It's an extremely helpful resource.

Overall, if your professor says something that seems a little too far-fetched or unconventional, it's completely acceptable to not take their word for it. It is a good and necessary thing to run your professor's

You should always respect your professors with your heart, but you should not always feel obligated to believe them with your mind.

statements through the grid of other scholarly perspectives on the subject. In fact, a truly respectable professor would encourage you to do that with their claims anyways.

How You Can Proceed

For some professors, their classroom is their arena, and their claims are their power plays. But at the same time, they're only as powerful as you allow them to be. So, receive your professors and their statements lightly. Realize they have a pronounced advantage in the classroom that they likely do not have in the larger academic realm.

This means you can be alert, but not alarmed.

And when it comes to their claims...

Listen well.
Critically analyze them.
Don't be paralyzed by them.   **Be alert, but not alarmed.**
Don't hesitate to test them.
And understand there's usually more to their claims than what you are currently hearing.

You should always respect your professors with your heart, but you should not always feel obligated to believe them with your mind. And with that, be at rest, exhale, smile, and enjoy the unique opportunity it is to be in a class where you can hear different perspectives for a change.

However, with any scholarly claim or assertion, there's often more to it than just a mere intellectual aspect. And that leads us right into Pointer #2.

THE HEART DWELLS BENEATH THE INTELLECT, THE LOGIC, AND THE EVIDENCE

"For the time will come when people will not put up with
sound doctrine. Instead, to suit their own desires, they
will gather around them a great number of teachers
to say what their itching ears want to hear."
- 2 Timothy 4:3

Have you ever said something to a friend, and then, instead of them understanding what you said, they actually interpreted your words in a way that was *completely different* from what you intended? I'm sure it's happened to you at some point.

In college, a similar experience happened to me when a group of friends and I were eating at one of our favorite fast food joints. Mid-way through the meal, I began feeling the pains of a double cheeseburger, corndog, quesadilla, and strawberry-banana-Oreo milkshake, and wheezed out, "Gracious, I need some exercise." But one of my friends, who has a much larger appetite for greasy carbohydrates, nodded his head and delightfully replied, "I agree, I need some extra fries, too." A puzzled look came over my face and I thought, "*What? I didn't say that.*" I kept eating, but then it hit me several minutes later: "*Oh... he thought I said 'extra fries'—not 'exercise'!*

How did that happen? Why did he hear 'extra fries' instead of 'exercise'? The apparent reason might be because they sound similar. But another reason might be because 'extra fries' was already on his mind, so he was hearing something he *wanted to hear* instead of what I *actually said*. It's possible that his hunger inclined his hearing.

In a similar way, the same can also be true in matters of intellect, logic, and evidence at the university level. The human heart—what it wants, prefers, and loves—can often screen information that is presented and choose information that is preferred. Preference is a powerful thing. It can often filter a host of information that comes our way, leaving us only with the things that we desire or find immediately plausible.

> *The human heart can often screen information that is presented and choose information that is preferred.*

The power of preference is a significant reality of the college experience. In fact, you can expect it to play out not only academically in the classroom with your professors, but also socially in the dormitory with your peers. Let's discuss how the power of preference affects these two significant spheres of university life.

Professors: The Heart Underneath Academics

We just discussed 1) *how* you can expect professors to treat you and 2) *what* you can expect them to teach you. But in this section, I want to look at the reasons for *why*. Ultimately, the reason for 'why' can be traced back to their heart, or bias.

Bias can be a loaded term, but it's essentially an opinion that has a particular slant because of certain, underlying preferences.

Let me give you a personal example.

I love the NBA team, the San Antonio Spurs. And when the Spurs play, I can be biased insofar as the referees are concerned. When a ref makes a call, I will always interpret the call through my preference of wanting the Spurs to win. I'll admit, too often, I will agree or disagree with a ref's call based on whether or not it favors the Spurs. Why? Because I *want* the Spurs to win more than I *want* the 'right' call to be made.

If it's a bad call—but it *favors* the Spurs—then I'll tell you it was the right call. If it's a good call—but it *doesn't* favor the Spurs—then I'll tell you it was the wrong call. In other words, I will disagree when I don't like how it affects my preferences, and I will agree when I like how it affects my preferences. Which means the main issue at play is never really the call itself, but my preference about what the call means to me. Go ahead, blow the whistle. Guilty as charged.

But that's how bias works: our judgment about certain information can be slanted because of our already-established preferences.

Now, the reality is that we all have bias. Your professors are biased, you are biased, and I am biased. It's part of being human. However, at the same time, you need to be aware of the inherent bias built into the classroom experience.

You should expect your professors to interpret and present information in a narrow, particular way.

Ultimately, you should expect your professors to interpret and present information in a narrow, particular way. Perhaps the most significant reason is because they *want* to see the information that way—possibly because it endorses their personal agenda, ideology, or lifestyle. A less significant reason may be because they feel like they *have* to teach the information that way—possibly because of their role at a secular university.

In terms of how this bias might operate in the classroom, I want you to think about how an undercurrent operates in the ocean. An undercurrent guides a large body of water in a certain direction because of a particular slant in the conditions, ultimately related to gravity, pressure-systems, or weather. In a similar way, the academic content of your classroom experience can sometimes be guided in a certain direction because of the undercurrent of your professor's preferences, ultimately related to lifestyle choices, values, or perspectives.

This undercurrent of preference is what makes me interpret a referee's call a certain way, and it's what can cause your professors to interpret information and evidence a certain way, too. The most significant factor, therefore, is never the call itself or the information itself, but the preference underneath about what it might mean to the person. Just like I will agree or disagree with a call based on how it best suits my preferences personally, it's likely for a professor to emphasize some information and dismiss other information, often because he likes or doesn't like what certain conclusions might mean to him individually. Typically, he will present what supports his bias, and he won't present what disagrees with his bias.

The natural consequence is that you may not hear other angles of scholarly opinion that hold just as much weight, if not more. And you may not know there even is 'another side' to an argument simply because it wasn't mentioned or, at the least, cast in a fair light.

But still, you might ask, *"Well, then how is it possible for a professor to actually do that? If the evidence for Christianity is so bulletproof, then*

how can professors teach something different? They wouldn't purpose-
fully teach something untrue."

Bias In Teaching

That's a great question. Ultimately, it's possible for professors to teach compellingly from secular points of view because of the way the academic realm is structured. Scholarship on any subject matter involves a vast collection of information. And in that vast collection, you will see several things:

- Information that *is* evidence.
- Information that *looks* like evidence.
- Conclusions that, therefore, *seem* to be competing.

Scholarship is essentially a mixed bag of 'relevant' information about a subject, not necessarily 'right' information about a subject. There are lots of findings, lots of hypotheses, and lots of information—but not all are legitimate.

Unfortunately, this means two things:

1. Because there is so much information available per topic, a certain view doesn't have to be credible in order for you to find it in the scholarly realm.
2. This also means the deck is stacked so that it's possible for your professors to choose the types of information and evidence they *want* to teach from.

All that is to say, many professors and students alike will not even consider the evidence for Christianity for two reasons. 1) From a spiritual standpoint, they don't *want* to believe it. 2) From an academic standpoint, they feel like they don't *have* to. Too often, they can get away with not considering Christianity simply because there *seems* to be so much competing information. In other words, if they want to have a certain perspective, they can likely find some 'scholarship' to arrive at that conclusion.

That's why you can have two different professors who are equally smart, but arrive at opposite ends of the spectrum when it comes to matters of faith. It's not primarily a matter of how their *brain* deals with the information, but how their *heart* approaches the information first.

Don't Christians Do That, Too?

I can already sense an objection: *"But don't Christians do the same thing? They prefer some information over other information because they want it to be true!"*

I see where this objection is coming from, however, that thought works from a false assumption: namely, that the Bible affirms the preferences of Christians and that Christians find their preferences reaffirmed in the Bible.

But that's not true. In fact, it's just the opposite. Not only is the Bible's doctrine uniquely counterintuitive (going against the grain of our natural logic), its ethics are also largely unpopular (going against the grain of our natural desires). The Bible offends our pride, and it challenges our sin. It

> *Christians don't believe in the Bible because it fits their preferences, but because they're convinced it's true.*

requires us to do things and believe things that fundamentally go against our natural preferences: giving our money away, saving sex for marriage, adhering to controversial stances on gender and sexuality, believing in Satan and hell, loving our enemies, and much more. Let's be honest, our natural selves hardly prefer *any* of those things. If anything, we'd prefer for those things to *not* be in the Bible.

Christians, however, don't believe in the Bible because it fits their preferences, but because they're convinced it's true. Christians don't look to the Bible to get their preferences reinforced, but transformed. That's an important distinction, and it's quite different from the way the world works.

> *Christians don't look to the Bible to get their preferences reinforced, but transformed.*

The world says, "Find truth that validates your preferences." But the Bible says, "Let Truth change your preferences." Christians, therefore, should approach information not because of how it might affect our preferences, but because we're committed to truth, despite our preferences.

Preference can play a powerful role when it comes to approaching scholarship, especially related to Christianity. In fact, one of the most renowned professors from my alma mater is proof of how preference can steer the intellect.

From Christian to Atheist

This professor is currently one of the world's leading scholars in anti-Christian thought. He's written numerous *New York Times* bestsellers attacking the validity of the Bible and Christianity. But what's interesting, however, is that *he was once an ordained minister.*

So what happened to him? How did he go from being a 'varsity level' Christian in full-time ministry to being a full-time destroyer of the Christian faith? Was it the alleged 2,000 errors in the New Testament? Was it a lack of archaeological support for biblical history? Was it skepticism in the reliability of the Bible? No. In fact, the real reason he left Christianity was not because of an *intellectual* reason, but because of a *preferential* reason. Namely, he didn't prefer what the Bible taught about suffering and hell. And now, surprisingly enough, it's those things he can't stand *preferentially* that fuel his academic endeavors to take down Christianity *intellectually.*

He will even admit that about himself, too. It's sad, but it conveys an important truth: the undercurrent of preference can determine where the ship of your intellectual convictions will end up.

Ultimately, if you want to find objections against Christianity and the Bible, you can and will find them. Because at the end of the day, your heart dwells beneath the intellect, the logic, and the evidence. And it will often screen what it wants to see and choose what it wants to believe. Truly, what the heart most wants, the mind will find most reasonable.[5]

> **What the heart most wants, the mind will find most reasonable.**

And in the college environment especially, what you'll realize is that most debates against Christianity are not so much about the evidence itself, but about what the heart does with what types of evidence are available. There's always underlying preferences that can tip the scales of your heart to prefer one side of scholarship to another side of scholarship.

Philosopher Blaise Pascal once famously said, "There is enough light for those who only desire to see, and enough obscurity for those who have a contrary disposition." In other words, for those who want truth, it will not be hard to find. But for those who do not want truth, it will be easy to dismiss. God is not coy. He's not hiding. If you want Him, He promises to come near to you (Ps. 9:10; Ja. 4:8). If you drop your preferences in humility and open your hands in desperation, He will show you truth. But if you don't want God—if you don't prefer His lordship in your life—then, of course, your preferences against Him will blind you from even seeing Him. And that goes for everyone.

Most debates against Christianity are not so much about the evidence itself, but about what the heart does with what types of evidence are available.

In terms of your professors, you need to recognize that their preferences will play a significant role in *how they teach* and in *what they teach*. When it comes to Christianity, it might be because they don't like what the Bible says about suffering, sexuality, gender, or money. It could be a number of preferential reasons.

However, preference doesn't merely affect professors; it affects students as well. In fact, the reasons for why some of your professors may teach from secular stances academically are the same reasons for why some of your peers may pursue a secular lifestyle socially, too. Let's look at a few of them.

Peers: The Heart Under Objections

As you already know, there are droves of Christians from youth groups who go off to college and all of a sudden stop believing in Christianity. I read a fascinating article recently that took a significant poll of these types of students, and interestingly, discovered that for a large majority, their forsaking of Christianity was never ultimately because of an intellectual reason.[6] It was, likewise, because of *new lifestyle preferences*. Being convinced by certain perspectives didn't lead them to adopt new lifestyle preferences; rather, new lifestyle preferences led them to adopt certain perspectives that supported their new lifestyle. A system of intellect didn't change the heart. The heart simply changed its system of intellect.

The article mentions that these 'pre-Christians'—students who have left the faith—will typically bring up intellectual objections for why they abandoned their faith. However, if they're honest, they'll admit that intellectual reasons were never *really* the root cause. More often than not, students confessed that intellectual objections were simply deployed as 'smokescreens' that they felt justified hiding behind while they pursued their lifestyle of choice in college. By suspending their Christian beliefs momentarily—and adhering to religious objections—it gave them the right to live the way they wanted to without feeling the convicting sting of their previously held Christian worldview.

College students today can find many reasons to deploy these intellectual 'smokescreens.'

One reason may be because these pre-Christians don't *prefer* the doctrine of Christianity any longer. It might be Christianity's stance on sexuality, hell, or exclusive salvation in Christ. However, they didn't abandon Christianity because it didn't make sense to them intellectually; rather, it just disagrees with their *preferences* now. And so, they find intellectual objections that, for the time being, endorse their current preferences and shelve their traditional convictions.

Another reason may be because they love approval and a sense of belonging more than Christ. And at college, they found a sense of approval and belonging with a type of community that just doesn't involve Christ. And so, they front intellectual objections for the time

> *Scholarship is essentially a mixed bag of 'relevant' information about a subject, not necessarily 'right' information about a subject.*

being that allow them to experience that sense of belonging they desire (however destructive it may be).

Or, it may be because they are enjoying sex outside of marriage, and they can't simultaneously believe in Christianity and have illicit sex without feeling a sharp sense of guilt. And so, for the time being, they find intellectual objections that remove the feelings of conviction so that they can more fully enjoy what they *really* want.

In many areas, college students will have a tendency to alleviate the tension between what they *want* versus what they've been taught by getting rid of their Christian belief system—one that disagrees with them, is irrelevant to them, or produces guilt—so that they can more fully enjoy the *preferences* of whatever it is they are involving themselves in, whether it is an unbiblical worldview, destructive sense of belonging, or new ethic on sex.

Indeed, it's much easier to adopt a set of intellectual objections on the mental level (even if you aren't totally convinced one way or another) than it is to wrestle with and submit to what Christianity requires on the heart level.

And for too many college students, not believing in Christianity has more to do with their lifestyle than their scholarship. Intellectual objections are more often smokescreens than the main issue. Their faith objections are not intellectual in origin, but preferential at the root. They are not a matter of the mind as much as they are a matter of the heart.

It's much easier to adopt a set of intellectual objections on the mental level than it is to wrestle with and submit to what Christianity requires on the heart level.

Truly, the mantra of the college culture is, "Follow your heart, and change your doctrine if necessary." But the Bible says, "Follow My Word, and your heart will change accordingly." No doubt, it can be easier to hide behind what you want to believe than it is to be convinced of what is actually true.

But Jesus did not say that what you want to be true will set you free. He said, "The truth will set you free" (Jn. 8:32). "Truly, truly, I say to you, everyone who practices sin is a slave to sin. ...So if the Son sets you free... *not your preferences*... you will be free indeed" (Jn. 8:34–36; italics mine).

For many college students, not believing in Christianity has more to do with their lifestyle than their scholarship.

The Root Issue

Overall, intellectual reasons are not always the root cause of a non-Christian worldview. The heart always lies behind the scholarship, and whatever 'scholarship' you *want* to believe in, you likely will so that it doesn't cause friction with your preferences.

English Reformer, Thomas Cranmer, hits the nail on the head quite profoundly:

"What the heart loves, the will chooses, and the mind justifies."[7]

That goes for everyone: for your professor, for your friends, and for yourself.

Intellectualism should never be sacrificed. It should be constantly pursued and refined. But beware of the heart. If you want to justify a lifestyle, you'll be able to find scholarship and intellectual objections that cater towards your preferences. In that sense, college is like a grocery store: if you want it, you can find it. But if you want truth, you can find just as many counter-objections that sufficiently prove secular claims wrong. And these counter-objections don't just come from Christian scholars, but from other secular scholars as well.

Truly, intellectual doubt can oftentimes be traced back to the heart more than the mind. But even then, intellectual doubt can still exist as a purely mental factor as well, and that leads us to Pointer #3: Don't Fear Doubt.

POINTER #3
DON'T FEAR DOUBT

Brothers, do not be children in your thinking.
Be infants in evil, but in your thinking be mature.
-1 Corinthians 14:20

Doubt, unfortunately, is readily looked down upon in many churches today. In fact, even with ourselves, our default mode is to immediately associate doubt with spiritual weakness—something to be ashamed of. Christians can hastily label doubt as shameful, but that's simply a shame.

The truth is, doubt does not have to be a bad thing. Doubt can simply represent a fundamental gap in your overall understanding of something—trying to reconcile what you *do know* with what you *don't know*, or with what you *don't yet know*.

Doubt can be an inherently *neutral* thing. How you *deal* with doubt, however, can either be a good thing or a bad thing.

In this chapter, I want to expose some of the unhealthy ways we often deal with doubt, and then I want provide some healthy ways we can deal with doubt instead. Then, in the next chapter, I'll highlight how God deals with both our doubt and the doubter in amazing and empowering ways.

The Unhealthy Approaches

Unhealthy approaches to doubt can ultimately be summed up as responding in *extremes*, treating doubt as if it was all or nothing. Either you accept doubt entirely or ignore doubt completely. Either you concede to it or cover over it. Either you throw your hands up in surrender or shrug your shoulders in resignation. The unhealthy approach does not allow for middle ground. Depending on who you are, you might respond to doubt in one of two ways: dramatically or apathetically. Let's look at each.

Unhealthy Approach #1
Dramatically, Conceding To It

First, the dramatic response to doubt essentially means to blow your doubt out of proportion. This response makes your doubt a much bigger deal than it actually is and gives it more significance than it actually deserves.

People who tend towards this approach to doubt are similar to impulsive drivers who rashly change lanes, swerving back and forth, in and out, again and again— according to which lane is fastest at the moment. Consistency, thoughtfulness, and caution on the road are considered inferior to getting a 1-2 second edge that may seem more efficient. But let's be honest: most of the time, this approach does more

A dramatic response to doubt would be to make doubt a bigger deal than it actually is and to give it more significance than it actually deserves.

to waste gas and sacrifice safety than it does to save time. It's reckless, and it often causes wrecks.

Likewise, the dramatic response to doubt is similar in that it immediately concedes to doubts based on what appears to be more intellectually compelling or efficient in the moment. It might involve doubting *everything* you have believed in the past based on *one* doubt you are wrestling with in the present.

The game Jenga can also serve as an effective image for this type of response to doubt. If you're unfamiliar with Jenga, it's a multi-player game involving a tall tower of 54 wooden blocks. The goal of the game is to take turns withdrawing blocks from the tower without causing it to topple over.

> *Doubt can simply represent a fundamental gap in your overall understanding of something.*

The game gets intense precisely because the tower is so top-heavy, and it becomes increasingly unstable as you remove blocks. All it takes is for someone to nudge one wrong block for the entire structure to come crashing down.

In a similar way, that's essentially what the dramatic response to doubt looks like. It assumes a type of faith that is top-heavy and unstable, and all it takes is for one doubt to nudge just *one* block of faith for the *entire* structure to come crashing down.

A practical example might be the thought, "*My professor said Genesis wasn't written by Moses; therefore, I can't trust the Bible at all.*" Or, "*My professor said the earth is 10 billion years old; therefore, the Bible must be completely untrustworthy.*"

Do you see a disturbing, irrational pattern in this line of thinking? The thought process hastily jumps from making a judgment on *one* issue of faith (Mosaic authorship for one book) to making a judgment on the *whole* issue of faith (legitimacy of the entire Bible). And it does so without even considering any other relevant pieces of information.

This is a dangerous thing to do because there's always more to the issue than what you may see at first. Don't perceive your faith like a Jenga tower, and don't let one doubt deliver a deathblow to the entirety of your faith.

The dramatic approach to doubt is too simplistic when approaching something as complex as the Bible and matters of faith. It's certainly wise to ruminate upon an assertion from a smart skeptic, but it's unwise to immediately concede. Responding to doubt in a dramatic fashion will be debilitating. You'll be building up and toppling down entire structures of worldview based on slight, momentary whims. You'll constantly be swerving in and out of lanes to fill those gaps in your understanding more quickly. But in the process, you'll be risking much more than the seconds you'll be saving. Overall, this approach to doubt is unhealthy. It's truly an anti-logical way of thinking and an anti-functional way of living.

> *It's certainly wise to ruminate upon an assertion from a smart skeptic, but it's unwise to immediately concede.*

Unhealthy Approach #2
Apathetically, Covering Over It

On the other hand, the apathetic response to doubt essentially means to diminish or ignore your doubt. This response sees your doubt as a much smaller deal than it actually is and gives it less significance than it actually demands. People who tend towards this approach to doubt typically prefer to live with a blind spot than to live with their head on a constant swivel of concern. They'd rather be blind and feel at peace than be aware and feel on edge.

An apathetic response to doubt would be to make doubt a smaller deal than it actually is and to give it less significance than it actually demands.

The apathetic response to doubt essentially represents the opposite of the dramatic response to doubt. If the dramatic response means to constantly swerve in and out of lanes (jumping to whatever seems compelling in the moment), the apathetic response would mean to never check for a more efficient lane (hardly considering any other alternate types of thought). If the dramatic response tends to be overly impulsive, then the apathetic response tends to be overly naïve. In the dramatic response, you may surrender your intellectual position. But in the apathetic response, you surrender your intellectual integrity altogether.

The apathetic response to doubt simply covers over doubt for the sake of keeping your current worldview in tact. It pretends doubt isn't there and disallows it from coming into contact with current beliefs.

Now, striving to keep your Christian worldview in tact is a good thing to pursue; however, ignoring your doubt in order to do so is not a good method to follow. At first, glossing over doubt might seem like an effective way—or even *spiritual* way—to deal with doubt. You might applaud yourself and think, "Well, *I didn't concede to doubt. I'm not like the person who's constantly changing their beliefs. At least I'm consistent.*" It's true, you didn't concede. But that doesn't necessarily mean the issue of doubt was resolved, either.

Imagine your doubt to be like a monster on the loose in your house. An apathetic response would look like pushing the monster in a closet, locking the door, and pretending it wasn't there. But does that approach really solve the problem? No. This is because the monster of doubt was never really addressed itself; instead, it was just confined for the time being. The approach might be an effective solution for the short-term, but it certainly isn't an effective approach for the long-term. That's because you just can't live in a house where there are scary, haunting noises continuously coming from the upstairs closet.

The monster of doubt may have chewed up and spit out the dramatic responders in an instant. But just because the apathetic responders locked the monster in the closet, that doesn't mean they are safe, either. This is because the anxiety of the monster will still gnaw away at them over time. Which means their faith may as well be just as dead as the dramatic responders who were consumed months ago. In either case, it's a lose-lose. In order to truly live at peace, you must confront that monster of doubt eventually.

Doubt can be an inherently neutral thing. How you deal with doubt, however, can either be a good thing or a bad thing.

Ultimately, the dramatic approach and the apathetic approach are unhealthy and ineffective ways of dealing with doubt. The irony is that while both approaches are opposites *in reaction*, they are actually two sides of the same coin *in essence*—because they both respond to doubt in extremes, both refuse to address the doubt in itself, and both resign to doubt in defeat.

Unfortunately, too many college students are tempted to fall into either of these categories, mainly because they think those are the only ways of responding to doubt after all. But that's not true. There's a healthy and effective way to respond to doubt: not conceding to it dramatically, not covering over it apathetically, but engaging with it effectively.

The Healthy Approaches

A healthier, balanced approach to doubt would be one that doesn't make too much of doubt or make too little of doubt, but rather, treats it with appropriate respect, thoughtfulness, and constraint—and engages with it accordingly. This approach is like a driver who checks his blind spots for oncoming traffic, but isn't afraid to change lanes when it is the safest and most reasonable thing to do.

This approach to doubt is not emotionally dramatic or apathetic, but rather, composed. It is not intellectually impulsive or naïve, but rather, sensible. It would allow doubt a fair hearing, but not an immediate verdict. It is one that is alert, but not alarmed.

Here are two practical action-steps you can take to approach doubt in a healthy way.

Healthy Approach #1
Screening for Gold

One healthy way to approach doubt is to treat it in the same way that a miner would screen for gold. For example, when a miner screens a particular area for gold, he brings all the elements of the soil into the screen of his filter. To be sure, no good miner immediately accepts all the elements of the soil *as* gold or immediately dismisses them all *not* as gold, either. Rather, the miner sifts through all the elements, not allowing any of them to go untouched without careful, meticulous analysis. In the process, the miner typically deems huge chunks of the deposit to be waste, re-categorizes smaller chunks of sediment for further investigation, and uncovers a handful of pieces that are garnished with those thrilling glitters of gold.

Similarly, when you are in class, strive to carry an intellectual 'screen' around with you. Take it all in, gather it all up. Don't immediately dismiss anything. But once you've taken it all in, don't let it all pass through. Because all of it is not gold. Sift and sift and sift, leaving no professorial claims or personal doubts untouched. Examine the quality of each. Roll it over in your mind. Test it against other sources. Hold it up to the light of Scripture. And for each, you have three options: 1) toss it, 2) re-categorize it for further investigation, or 3) get richer in mind, heart, and soul.

> **Allow your doubts to be balanced for consideration, but don't let them tip the scale of your convictions all at once, either.**

Allow your doubts to be balanced for consideration, but don't let them tip the scale all at once, either. In every mountain of doubt, there's likely to be several nuggets of gold. So don't bypass the mountains and miss out on the gold. Bring your screen with you on the journey. Overall, you'll be thankful that you committed the time to something so valuable.

Healthy Approach #2
Using Ju-Jitsu

A second healthy way to approach your doubt would be to engage it with the technique of Ju-Jitsu. Not that you should swing your fists at it, but rather, *how* you should fight it.

Do you know what makes Ju-Jitsu different from Taekwondo or Karate or any other martial art? It's distinct because it teaches a smaller person how to defend himself against a larger opponent by using *leverage*. It's essentially the technique of using the opponent's own force against himself rather than confronting him with your own force.[8]

In the same way, we must use leverage when we struggle with doubt. When doubt lunges at us with questions, unknowns, and skepticism, we need to leverage those same things against it. A healthy way to approach doubt would be to engage it in same the way that it engages you. Let me give you an illustration.

If you're a 150-lb scrub and you're in the ring with a 250-lb boxer, what's the best approach you could take (besides running away)? If the boxer throws a punch at you, it would seem unwise to 1) lunge forward at him or 2) absorb the punch from him. We both know the match would end in a swift knockout. The technique of Ju-Jitsu, however, appeals to using leverage as an effective solution. How so? Because the force of momentum that your opponent creates on his own accord is of much greater power than any punch you could muster up in your own strength. Which means your greatest advantage would be to use his power against himself, instead of trying to fight him in your own strength.

When the boxer lunges a powerful punch at you, an effective strategy may be to side step the punch—with his momentum striving towards you—and stick your foot out and trip him. Trip him in his stride. Make him trip over the force of his own momentum. In fact, the greater his momentum, the more effective your trip. But all you did was stick your foot out. You didn't have to be strong to do that. You just put yourself in a position to leverage his momentum, his force, and his power against himself. And look, you—the weaker fighter—are now the one standing over him in advantage. Good job, 150-lb scrub. You did it.

That picture somewhat resembles how you can effectively duel with doubt, too. It's not unusual to feel small, weak, and unmatched against the larger, looming opponent of doubt. When you're face-to-face with doubt in the ring of life, you might need to implement the leverage principle of Ju-Jitsu in order to gain confidence over it.

But practically, what does that look like? How can you fight doubt by leveraging its power against itself? Here is the answer:

By doubting your doubts.

By questioning your questions.

By being skeptical of your skepticism.

It means to doubt your doubts in the same proportion that your doubts cause you to doubt your beliefs. It involves questioning your questions to the same degree that your questions lead you to question your convictions. It looks like being just as skeptical towards your skepticism as your skepticism causes you to be skeptical of your rationale.

When doubts lunge towards you in great strength, you can respond by doubting your doubts—using the power it poses against you, against it. Indeed, by doubting your doubts, you will essentially cause your doubts to trip over its own momentum. And as a result, you will feel more in control, more at peace, and not as unsettled.

Don't give your doubts an unfair advantage by not doubting them just as much as they're causing you to doubt what you believe. Otherwise, you've already conceded that they are truer than your current convictions and beliefs. But you don't know that. Which means your doubts deserve to be doubted. They are, after all, shadowy doubts, not substantiated truths. So don't let them wrestle *you* down. Wrestle *them* down, and do it with the same power they use against you, just like Ju-Jitsu. That's a healthy, fair, and effective way to respond to doubt.

> *Don't give your doubts an unfair advantage by not doubting them just as much as they're causing you to doubt what you believe.*

Gaining Confidence and Peace

When you screen your doubt and when you doubt your doubt, you put doubt back in its rightful place. You won't make doubt out to be a bigger deal than it really is (dramatic approach), and you won't make it out to be a smaller deal than it actually is, either (apathetic approach). Rather, you will have observed it correctly, treated it properly, and handled it accordingly. This is the way of gaining confidence and peace—as you struggle with doubt and as you claim victory over doubt.

> *When you screen your doubt and when you doubt your doubt, you put doubt back in its rightful place.*

Overall, doubt is not a bad thing. In fact, it can be a good thing if approached in the right way. Therefore, see your doubt as a launch pad that you can use to jump into the gaps of your understanding and to fill those gaps with truth, reason, and experience. See it as a prime opportunity to make your faith even stronger than before.

Don't fear your doubt. Don't waste your doubt. Leverage your doubt.

By doing so, you'll arrive at greater, richer experience of faith.

At the same time, our struggle with doubt can be more than just an inward, mental battle. Outward, social pressures can also contribute to how we struggle with doubt, too. We'll discuss this more in Pointer #4.

GOD WELCOMES THE DOUBTER, BUT CHALLENGES THE DOUBT

"Put your finger here; see my hands.
Reach out your hand and put it into my side.
Stop doubting and believe."
–Jesus (John 20:27)

In the last chapter, we discussed that we shouldn't treat doubt as if it's a bad thing, nor should we be frightened of it, either. This is because doubt can merely represent the gap between *what we do know* with *what we don't know*, or with *what we don't yet know*. In fact, in many ways, doubt can be a good thing for the way that it stretches and strengthens the muscle of our faith.

In this chapter, however, we will explore the different ways **people/ institutions** typically deal with us when we doubt (and why their conventional approaches fail us in general), and then we will look at how **God** deals with us when we doubt (and why his approach in particular comforts and empowers us).

Often, we can fear expressing our doubts because of how we might be viewed by the people around us. We may think our *church* would deal with us harshly if we expressed our doubts. We may think our *family* would treat us differently if we voiced doubts. We may even treat *ourselves* bitterly if we honestly admitted our doubts. And we may think *God* would treat us harshly if we expressed doubts, too.

But that certainly isn't the case when we look at Scripture. In the next several pages, I want to show how God truly deals with us when we doubt—because if we only knew, we'd find a type of power that would strengthen us to confidently stand up under the burdens our doubt can heap upon us.

What's so striking—and immensely encouraging—is that most(!) of the greatest leaders in the Bible experienced life-long bouts of intense doubt.

Abraham. Moses. Joseph. David. Paul.

Yet, they became renowned as people of great faith—not because they never doubted—but because they came to know who God was to them when they doubted... and found the power to overcome.

Likewise, we don't become spiritual giants by never doubting. We become spiritual giants by experiencing how God deals with us when we doubt. Only that will empower us to deal with our doubt in a way that is fruitful.

> *We don't become spiritual giants by never doubting. We become spiritual giants by experiencing how God deals with us when we doubt.*

In college, you will generally observe the influences of how two conventional groups deal with the doubter as a person and with doubt as a topic:

The Conservatives, which is *possibly* your church.
The Liberals, which is *probably* your university.

But as we will see, both groups tend to be unsympathetic towards the doubter and provide rather ineffective solutions for doubt. Only a third option—how God deals with us when we doubt—gives sympathy to the doubter and solutions to the doubt. Let's first take a look at why the two conventional ways (conservatism and liberalism) of dealing with the doubter *don't work*, and then let's see why the unconventional way God deals with the doubter *does work*.

How Conservatives Deal with the Doubter

The Conservative culture, which might be representative of your church background, tends to perceive doubt as something to be ashamed of and avoided at all costs. It brazenly says, '*Whatever you do, just don't doubt!*' In this way, the Conservative culture seems to put a premium on saving face over solving issues.

The Conservative culture seems to put a premium on saving face over solving issues.

But this viewpoint doesn't help the doubter or the doubt for a couple of different reasons.

First, the Conservative culture can produce communal tension. When people are part of a culture that isn't sensitive to doubt, they grow fearful and dejected when they *do* doubt. This is because their doubt becomes more than just an issue of doubt: it becomes an issue of identity and community. It doesn't just represent an obstacle in their mind, but becomes an obstacle to their sense of value and belonging. Voicing one's doubt might not only make them feel inferior as a community member, but it might also mean jeopardizing their sense of acceptance from their core community, too. Therefore, doubters don't just fear doubt in this culture, but what that doubt might possibly lead to—isolation and rejection.

Second, the Conservative culture can also produce personal stress. When people are in a community that isn't sympathetic to doubt, it essentially tells its members that they should bottle up their struggles. But these people and their doubts hardly get better.

Think about what happens with a volcano. Lava from the Earth's core gushes upward and creates pressure right beneath the Earth's crust. The more lava that flows to the surface, the greater the pressure is exerted on the surface. And if the lava keeps flowing and the pressure keeps increasing, one of two things will eventually happen: 1) the surface will erupt dramatically, or 2) the surface will disintegrate subtly from underneath. The pressure's got to give somehow.

Likewise, when we bottle up our doubts—instead of expressing them to others or striving to work through them—our faith becomes highly pressurized. And it will usually lead to one of two inevitable results: 1) an eruption of religious frustration that can be evident to all, or 2) the creation of a release valve that can alleviate the tension without others knowing. When doubts and struggles go unchecked, people either end up detonating in despair, publicly revoking their faith, or they end up channeling their frustrations in secret, privately compromising their faith.

In college, you'll see both of these things happen. Some of your Christian friends will feel the intense pressure of trying to be someone they're supposed to be for family, friends, church, or God—and they'll explode. To them, religious expectation will feel like too much pressure to live up to, so in response, they'll push religion away as much as they can. They might hit the party scene hard for a season, or they might give up their faith altogether.

Other Christian friends may feel the same pressure as well, except they'll play the 'Christian' role in public, yet maintain a secret 'release valve' for doubts or sinful living in private. To them, religious expectation will feel like a necessary pressure, so matters of faith will feel more like a job to keep up than a joy to live out. These Christians may look spiritually 'polished' on the outside, but on the inside, they're struggling. Because they feel like they can't voice their issues, questions, or concerns to others, those things continue to build up a destructive pressure over time.

The Conservative culture has a tendency to tell people that they should bottle up their doubts for the sake of looking like a polished Christian; but that kind of pressure will usually lead someone to the brink of eruption or compromise. And that's exactly why Conservatism particularly frustrates Christians in college. It's seen to hastily supply answers, but not provide the time or space for its members to vulnerably express their struggles. It can often be accused of dealing with complex struggles in narrow, shallow ways— like applying Band-Aids of pat answers upon gaping wounds of doubt. It's often heavy on truth, heavy on the 'ought's,' but too light on empathy. It can feel like a hammer, making every issue out to be a nail. And by applying the pressures of expectation, it essentially treats a doubting Christian like a volcano: causing him to explode suddenly and dramatically, or causing him to crumble from underneath.

The Conservative culture doesn't do justice to the doubter because it says you cannot be emotionally or intellectually authentic while at the same time being a genuine Christian.

Overall, the Conservative culture doesn't do justice to the doubter because it basically says that *you cannot be emotionally or intellectually authentic while at the same time being a genuine Christian.*[9] This culture isn't sympathetic to the doubter as a person, nor does it provide thoughtful solutions to the doubt as an issue. It just doesn't work.

How Liberals Deal with the Doubter

On the other hand, the Liberal culture, which likely represents your university, treats doubt as something to be embraced and pursued in itself. It is perceived as intellectually sophisticated and emotionally mature. It brashly says, '*Doubt absolutely everything!*' It puts a premium on free thinking over truth finding.

The Liberal culture essentially urges you to always be in doubt about everything—to be skeptical, to be cynical, and to have unresolved, eternal doubt about every aspect of life.[10] This is most likely the philosophical approach you will hear from your professors.

> *The Liberal culture seems to put a premium on free thinking over truth finding.*

However, this Liberal viewpoint falls short in certain regards.

First, the reality is that it's simply impossible to be doubtful about absolutely everything. For example, if you say you can doubt everything, but don't doubt that very statement, you're actually giving yourself an exemption that isn't fair. Tim Keller says, "You cannot doubt everything, and at the same time, doubt your own skepticism about everything. If you refuse to doubt your own doubt itself, you aren't being consistent in your own philosophy—you're just picking and choosing."[11] The irony is that the Liberal culture refuses to doubt its own doubtfulness. It says, "*There are no absolutes! You can't be sure about anything!*" But that very statement, of course, asserts an absolute assurance about *that* belief. It's intellectual hypocrisy.

Second, it's simply impossible to actually live in a reality of total doubt. Not only is it intellectually impossible, it's also practically impossible and largely delusional.

If the Liberal culture was consistent in their beliefs, they would doubt their sense of skepticism... however, they are hesitant to do so. This is because as soon as they doubt their doubtfulness, they've become open to the possibility of real knowledge and real truth. And a main problem of the Liberal culture is that underneath a sense of doubting everything can sometimes be the fear of knowing something. But why would anyone fear knowing something? Because once you know truth, you are held accountable to it. Too many people in the Liberal culture don't *want* to know anything because that means they won't *have* to be held accountable to anything.

> *Once you know truth, you are held accountable to it.*

While this culture is applauded for being vulnerable and seeking truth, they're surprisingly notorious for not wanting to arrive at truth after all. But the truth is, you just can't live in a reality without commitments, knowledge, or truth. It would be like an architect working on a project without numbers, materials, or property. You simply have to live in a world of knowledge. When your car runs out of fuel, it actually does. When your bank account has $300, it actually does. When you eat nothing but sugar, you actually are. You can't second-guess your reality and entertain the possibility that your car is full of gas, or that your bank account is actually $300,000, or that you're actually eating vegetables. We are accountable to the way our car works, bank account works, and health works. And issues of biblical truth, moral principle, and ethical concepts are no different.

The Liberal culture certainly baits many college students with the appeal of intellectual sophistication and low accountability, but it actually proves to be rather frustrating and immensely unsatisfying over time, no matter who you are—Christian or non-Christian. This is because it allows its members the freedom to feel vulnerable with their struggles (which is great!), but it doesn't ever give any answers to their questions (which is important!).

The Liberal culture might approach your doubts with sympathy, but it doesn't give resolution to your doubts. It's often heavy on empathy and heavy on the 'what's,' but it's light on truth. If the Conservative culture creates volcanoes out of people because of intense pressure, the Liberal culture creates clouds out of people because of absolutely no pressure at all. These members just float intellectually adrift according to the ever-changing principles and conditions of the culture around them.

Overall, the Liberal culture doesn't do justice to the doubter because it essentially says that *there's no truth anyways, so being a Christian implies ignorance and arrogance.* The problem is, this culture doesn't actually resolve your doubt—it just seeks to resolve your emotional and intellectual struggle by normalizing doubt. But normalizing a struggle does not cure a struggle. This culture isn't sympathetic to the doubter as a person, and it doesn't provide thoughtful solutions to the doubt as an issue. It just doesn't work.

Conservatism vs. Liberalism

As such, both the Conservative and Liberal cultures fall short in actually helping the doubter from a holistic standpoint.

Conservative culture emphasizes truth, but doesn't give you the grace to struggle. Liberal culture emphasizes grace to struggle, but gives you no truth. Conservative culture challenges the doubt, but doesn't welcome the doubter. Liberal culture welcomes the doubter, but doesn't challenge the doubt.

The Conservative approach might soothe the mind, but it will certainly crush the heart. The Liberal approach might soothe the heart, but it will certainly frustrate the mind.

Conservatives think the solution is to help the mind. But if you don't help the heart, you actually don't help the mind as much as you think. And Liberals think the solution is to help the heart. But if you don't help the mind, you actually don't help the heart as much as you think.

Ultimately, the Conservative approach and the Liberal approach are *polar opposites* in terms of how they deal with doubter. However, what's so ironic is that both are *exactly identical* in terms of what they ultimately deliver. Neither approach gives sympathy to the doubter or resolution to the doubt. Both are equally unsympathetic to your emotional hurt and unhelpful to your intellectual struggles.

> *Conservative culture challenges the doubt, but doesn't welcome the doubter. Liberal culture welcomes the doubter, but doesn't challenge the doubt.*

But thankfully, they are not the only options. There is a third approach, and that is how God deals with you as you deal with doubt.

How God Deals with the Doubter

Christianity, in stark contrast to the conventional methods of society, displays a surprisingly balanced, sympathetic, and refreshing approach to the doubter. The God of the Bible provides real help and real answers, and He does so by critiquing the coldness of Conservatism and deflating the fancifulness of Liberalism.

One place we see this is in the life of Abraham, the 'Father of Faith.' Throughout his entire life, Abraham consistently doubts God's promises and pleads with God time and time again, "God...*how can I really, truly, actually know? How can I really be sure?*"

But how does God respond to Abraham each time?

Does God take on the demeanor of a Conservative drill sergeant and say, "*How dare you question me! Pitiful!*"—No, never. Or does God take on the demeanor of Liberal hippie professor and say, "*Well, yeah, that's the way it is. Groovy. Embrace doubt as ultimate reality, you'll never know.*"—No, God doesn't respond that way, either.[12]

God responds to Abraham beautifully each time. God gives Abraham assurances of his loving faithfulness to him as a doubter, and He gives Abraham signs of his provision to him for his doubts. God provided a covenant when Abraham doubted His plan (Gen. 15); God provided a son in old age when Abraham doubted His promise (Gen. 21); and God provided the ram in the thicket when Abraham doubted His purpose (Gen. 22). God entered into Abraham's doubt by *sympathizing with him*, and then He challenged Abraham's doubt by *providing for him*.

You can also see this same approach in the famous interaction between 'Doubting' Thomas and the resurrected Jesus. Thomas says, "*Unless I see in his hands the mark of the nails, and place my finger into the mark of the nails, and place my hand into his side, I will never believe"* (Jn. 20:25).

And how does Jesus respond to Thomas?

Does Jesus take the Conservative 'beat-down' approach and simply tell him to suck it up and stop doubting? No. Does Jesus take the Liberal 'give-up' approach and simply tell him he'll just have to deal with never knowing completely? No. Rather, *Jesus actually gives Thomas what he asked for and shows him the scars in his hands and the scar on his side.*[13] When Thomas questioned and doubted, Jesus responded in beautiful grace and astonishing truth.

It's easy to think that doubting God is inherently sinful. But if doubting is such a sinful thing to do, then why does Jesus give Thomas what he asks for? It's because he cares for us, and our struggles matter to him. Through this interaction, Jesus shows us that God does not accuse us for our doubts; God welcomes us with our doubts. But significantly, however, Jesus doesn't stop there. Jesus shows Thomas the nail prints, and then boldly declares, *"Now stop doubting and believe"* (Jn. 20:27). Jesus didn't give Thomas every answer, but he did give him the sufficient ones. [14] And God does the same for us.

On one hand, God does not condemn doubt, but on the other hand, He does not condone doubt. Instead, He challenges doubt. He demonstrates a fascinating balance to us when we doubt such that our

> **God welcomes our doubts as they are, but He does not welcome them to stay as they are.**

doubts are welcomed as they are, but they're not welcomed to stay as they are. He never encourages us to doubt, but doubters are always completely welcomed and addressed.[15]

Unlike the Conservative approach, He declares, "I love you, even when you doubt." He cares for us in our emotional struggles. And unlike the

Liberal approach, He declares, "There are answers, and I will help you." He cares for us holistically in our intellectual struggles.

So when you express doubt and say, "*My faith is weak!*" God doesn't do the Conservative thing and say, "*How dare you doubt!*" and God doesn't do the Liberal thing and say, "*This is just the way it is!*" Instead, He says, "*This is the way to give you a masterful life. I will give you more faith, and I will grow you. Doubters are welcome because honest admissions of weakness, difficulty, and struggle are the way you grow.*"[16]

> **Honest admissions of weakness, difficulty, and struggle are the way you grow.**

Ultimately, God paves a highway where Conservatism and Liberalism both dead-end. Conservatism paves a lane for finding truth, but dead-ends when it comes to providing grace. Liberalism paves a lane for providing grace, but dead-ends when it comes to finding truth. But in Christianity, God opens up an expressway of both grace and truth that never dead-end. He offers us extravagant grace for the heart and abundant truth for the mind, sufficient for wherever we are in the journey of life.

As we navigate through the college environment, let's take God at his word. Let's approach him like Abraham, the Father of Faith, and like Thomas, the Disciple of Doubts—giving him our 'Isaacs' and taking hold of his nail-pierced hands. When it's all said and done, we will look back and realize that our doubts were as empty as the tomb He overcame.

"I believe; help my unbelief!"
(Mark 9:24)

POINTER #5

THE RESURRECTION OF CHRIST IS YOUR CONFIDENCE

And if Christ has not been raised, then our preaching
is in vain and your faith is in vain.
-1 Corinthians 15:14

It would only be fitting to follow the chapters discussing the doubts a Christian *can have* with a chapter devoted to the confidence a Christian *must have.*

When we are struggling with doubt, we can use healthy approaches to doubt versus unhealthy approaches to doubt, and we can trust who God is to us and how God deals with us when we doubt. But nevertheless, the reality of doubt—in terms of its lack of answers—can still remain.

So you might ask, *"What hope do I have as far as answers are con-cerned? God gave Abraham a ram in the thicket, and Thomas a view of his nail-scarred hands. What does God give me when I doubt? Sure, I can use healthy ways of coping with doubt, and I can trust God with my doubts... but at the same time, I can't just not have any answers!!"*

And you are absolutely right.

On one hand, God *will* give you answers along your way to finding truth. But on the other hand, how do you possess a general confidence in the truth of Christianity while you search for those answers to your particular questions? What gives you some sort of intellectual and emotional anchor while you get thrown around in the waves of uncertainty from time to time?

The answer is the resurrection of Jesus Christ.

This truth lies at the bedrock of the Christian faith, and it is your anchor of absolute confidence when everything else seems so uncertain.

To be up front, I am not going to tell you every reason for why the resurrection is true. Rather, I am going to tell you why the truth of the resurrection can give you every reason to have peace with everything else.

The truth is, the Bible doesn't resolve all of our questions or soothe all of our doubts—but it does give resolution and peace to the main ones. And that means we can have peace with the unresolved, minor ones.

The Bible doesn't resolve all of our questions or soothe all of our doubts—but it does give resolution and peace to the main ones.

Often, we think that if we can't answer all parts of said topic, then we can't be confident at all. But that's simply not the case. Feeling like we need to be absolutely assured in every category of our belief may seem like an admirable approach, but it will cause burnout if we insist to have every single answer, especially all at once.

This is because having all the answers isn't necessary.

In fact, having all the answers isn't even possible.

The reality is that there are truths of primary, central significance.

And then there are other truths of secondary, peripheral significance.

That's true about virtually everything in life.

In other words, just because you can't know everything about something doesn't mean you can't be sure about anything. It's totally acceptable to wrestle with secondary truths while simultaneously holding fast to primary truths. In fact, it's a certainty in the primary truths that often keeps you anchored when the secondary truths seem adrift.

And for the Christian, the most foundational, primary truth is the resurrection of Jesus Christ. Being assured of the resurrection will keep you anchored and confident when you battle uncertainty with anything else.

> *Being assured of the resurrection will keep you anchored and confident when you battle uncertainty with anything else.*

Jenga Tower vs. Pyramid

Think back to when we compared our faith to a Jenga tower. We discussed that it's an inaccurate, dangerous metaphor precisely because it's so unstable: it has a base that's just as narrow as its top. If you remove any piece of the tower, the entire thing could topple over. The problem with the Jenga tower is that any block—top to bottom—could be as critically important as the next.

But our faith is not like not that. It does not treat every idea with the same level of importance. Some truths are more foundational than others.

A more accurate way of understanding our faith, however, is to view it like a *pyramid* instead. A pyramid, unlike a Jenga tower, has a wide foundation and a narrow top, which makes it more stable. A pyramid is a triangular structure with a gradient of layers—some larger and some smaller. The larger layers are foundational to the smaller layers, and therefore, provide stability for the smaller layers.

Similarly, our faith resembles the structure of a pyramid because it has a base of large, foundational commitments upon which other, smaller commitments are built upon. At the very bottom are the most important truths, and at the very top are convictions of lesser importance. The most important truths aren't affected by the lesser important truths. In fact, it's a confidence in the larger, essential truths that provides stability when the smaller, nonessential truths are challenged.

Some truths are more foundational than others.

Christianity's most important truths would include the Trinity and the resurrection of Christ. Convictions of lesser importance might include a certain view on baptism or the age of the earth.

It's extremely important to understand parts of your faith in terms of primary truths and secondary truths. Here's why:

Say, for example, a professor claims the earth is 10 billion years old, but your view of the earth is 10,000 years old. His claim can potentially affect you in one of two different ways, depending on your 'type' of faith.

If you have a 'Jenga tower' type of faith, you'd be tempted to equate the age of the earth and the resurrection of Christ as equally important ideas. So, hearing that the earth is 10 billion years old would shake the entirety of your faith.

But, if you have a 'pyramid' type of faith, you would treat the resurrection of Christ as a primary truth and the age of the earth as a secondary truth. So, hearing that the earth is 10 billion years old would not shake the entirety of your faith—it would just challenge a small piece of it.

By making a distinction between primary and secondary convictions,

Your faith should look more like a pyramid than a tower.

you can be open to the idea of the earth being either young or old without it shaking your entire faith. Why? Because a 10,000 year-old earth or a 10 billion year-old earth doesn't make Christianity any less true. The foundation of Christianity is the resurrected Christ, not the surmised age of the earth. So, hearing that the earth is 10 billion years old will not shake your faith because the foundation of your faith won't be shaken. Your peripheral belief might be challenged, but your central belief will stay secure.

The problem with a 'Jenga tower' type of faith is that *any* doubt can poke loose *any* block of faith and threaten the entire thing. But that's not the case with a 'pyramid' type of faith because it distinguishes between primary truths and secondary truths. While doubt may challenge some truths, it won't be able to threaten the entire structure.

And for the Christian, the resurrection of Jesus Christ exists as the foundation upon which everything else finds its ultimate support. It gives us a strong sense of stability and peace when other beliefs are challenged. Therefore, if there's one thing to have the answer for, and if there's one thing you can be certain of—it's the resurrection of Jesus Christ.

> *The resurrection of Jesus Christ exists as the foundation upon which everything else in Christianity finds its ultimate support.*

The Resurrection Is Your Reason For Trust

You don't have to be an astute theologian to defend the resurrection, nor do you have to be an acclaimed apologist to prove it. Anyone who looks at the evidence and weighs the reasonableness for the resurrection can be absolutely assured that *it did happen*. That's a bold statement, but it has not been, and will not be, disproven.

In fact, it is so compelling that many atheist scholars don't even touch the subject in debates. They tend to discuss other issues, such as the 'problem of evil' or 'alleged errors in the Bible.' Many scholars resort to writing off the resurrection as absurd—not because it lacks intellectual warrant, but because it requires personal commitment if acknowledged. They don't consider it because they don't want to come to grips with the possibility that it's true. Because if it is true, then it requires a rather significant response—one that many people don't prefer to make. As such, it's more of an uncomfortable topic that people would rather bypass than actually engage in.

> *Many scholars resort to writing off the resurrection as absurd—not because it lacks intellectual warrant, but because it requires personal commitment if acknowledged.*

However, the intellectual support for the resurrection of Christ is not just compelling, but overwhelmingly so. We'll discuss a handful of those reasons in the following pages.

Ultimately, when you encounter doubt or grapple with questions about Christianity, the most important thing you can do is to anchor your confidence in the resurrection of Christ. Every argument and every doubt pales in comparison to the substantiality of the resurrection. Why? Because if the resurrection is true, then it doesn't matter what argument you hear, or what doubt you have, or what claims your professor makes against Christianity. At the end of the day, if the resurrection is true, Jesus *is* who he says he is and Christianity *is* objective truth.

Now, this doesn't mean all of your questions will immediately dissolve.

This simply means you can have peace while you struggle through hard questions. The certainty of the resurrection can be to you a solid ground beneath your feet as you strive to move forward through the mist and fog of uncertainties. Practically speaking, this means you can trust God with your doubts.

If the resurrection is true, Jesus is who he says he is and Christianity is objective truth.

You can trust God with the lesser things you don't know, like your doubts, based on the most important thing you can know, which is the resurrection. You can trust God with what you can't understand or can't find proof for based on what you can understand and can find proof for: namely, that He is the resurrected Lord who holds in his hands both reality and every answer that seems difficult to find right now.

When you can't be absolutely sure of everything in your faith, you can be absolutely sure of the resurrection of Jesus Christ. And that should give you peace in your struggles. It is the rock, the central truth you can stand on in the midst of rather hazy, peripheral questions.

Objections & Responses

Unfortunately, discussing every objection, answer, proof, and rationale in support of the resurrection is simply beyond the scope of this small book. However, it would be unfair to not provide some brief reasons in support of the resurrection, too. So here are some common objections you might hear and some ways you might be able to respond.

Objection: *"People thought they saw the resurrected Jesus, but they were just hallucinating."*

This is a common objection, but the Apostle Paul addresses it by recounting an event where Jesus publicly appeared before a crowd of 500 (1 Co. 15). The objection that people hallucinated and saw Jesus might hold weight if it were only a couple of people, or if the experience had only happened behind closed doors. But this public, eyewitness account communicates quite the opposite. It says that 500 people testified to seeing Jesus in public. It's true that some people can hallucinate. But 500 people do not all hallucinate at the same time, each one having the exact same experience. In addition, since it happened in public, it would be quite easy for others to refute if it didn't happen.

> *500 people do not all hallucinate at the same time, each one having the exact same experience.*

Objection: *"The disciples could have gotten confused and gone to the wrong tomb."*

This may seem like a probable situation, but in reality, it would have been really difficult for the disciples to mistake Jesus' tomb for someone else's. Why? Because Jesus' tomb would have been the only tomb surrounded by an entire garrison of Roman soldiers. Not many people have an army surrounding their tomb. However, Jesus did because both Roman Empire and the Jewish establishment wanted to prevent someone from stealing the body.

Objection: *"Jesus actually didn't die, so he didn't actually resurrect."*

This objection is also known as the swoon theory, alluding to the idea that Jesus passed out under trauma, but didn't die. However, the credibility of this notion fails when held up to the details of what is reported in the gospel accounts. For example, we read that blood and water flowed from Jesus' side when he was speared (Jn. 19:34). Back then, they didn't recognize a separation of blood and water to indicate death, but today's science would quickly identify that as a primary indicator.

Additionally, assuming that Jesus was beaten to the point of death—but did not actually die—and then escaped from a tomb surrounded by an army seems highly implausible. He would have had to roll a "very large"/ "great" stone (Mt. 27:60, Mk. 16:4) away from the entrance of the tomb, and then either stealthily elude or single-handedly take on a fleet of Rome's most highly trained

It would have been impossible to confuse Jesus' tomb with someone else's, because his tomb would have been the only one surrounded by Roman soldiers.

soldiers stationed right outside (Mt. 27:62-66). No one—who was crucified on a cross, beaten to the point where he looked dead, and partook of no food or water for the next 3 days—could ever have accomplished a physical feat such as that.

Objection: "*The body of Jesus was stolen once it was placed in the tomb. People just assumed a resurrection because the body was missing.*"

This is a great objection, too. One of my favorite details in the resurrection account, however, is that the disciples noticed that the burial cloths used to wrap Jesus were *folded* neatly on the headstone (Jn. 20:7). Now, that begs a couple questions:

1) If you were stealing a deceased body, why would you unwrap him before you stole him? Personally, I'd rather not touch the decomposing parts of a brutally tortured dead person as I'm moving him from point A to point B.

2) The act of robbery happens in a rush. You have a tight time frame to thieve and to leave without being caught. If you were stealing the dead body of someone famous, you would probably be in a hurry... especially if you're trying to evade a group of Rome's most skilled soldiers. If you're in

a rush, why take the time to neatly fold the dead guy's clothes before leaving? It would seem foolish to do so. Therefore, since the burial cloths were folded, it reinforces the notion that Jesus' body was not stolen.

Objection: *"The disciples could have made up the whole thing."*

This is perhaps the strongest objection, and one that I personally struggled with for some time. But there are 2 evidences that compellingly deny it.

> *The folded burial cloths reinforce the notion that Jesus' body was not stolen.*

First, if the entire story were simply made up, it would have been extremely easy for other people to refute it. The Christian story largely took place in the public square for all to witness; it did not happen in a private cave that one person experienced, like Islam. Therefore, if something didn't happen as the gospel writers recounted, then anyone could have easily come out and said, "No! *That absolutely did not happen! That's a lie.*" However, no one in history ever came forward with refutations. And to be sure, there certainly were people in power who would have had every motive to come up with refutations, too. The Romans and the Jews both hated Jesus and would have loved to refute the veracity of these stories. Or even make up refutations against it for that matter.

However, they didn't. And that's because the Jewish leaders and Roman leaders encountered Jesus in the public square along with everyone else. They couldn't have said the gospel accounts were fabricated—and they couldn't have made up their own false narratives—because the common folk would have been able to refute their claims with their own eyewitness experience. The gospel records survived because what was written down could be backed up by eyewitness experience from a host of all types of people.

Second, the gospel accounts record that women were the first to witness the empty tomb of the resurrected Christ. That might seem to be an insignificant detail to our modern perspective. However, the gospel accounts were written in a patriarchal (male-dominated) society, so this detail would have significantly stuck out to its modern day readers. In that day, women's testimonies were considered much less trustworthy than a man's. In fact, in a court of law, the testimony of 3 women equaled the testimony of 1

You can trust God with the lesser things you don't know, like your doubts, based on the most important thing you can know, which is the resurrection.

man. When the gospel writers communicated that the first people to witness the empty tomb were 2 women, it would have been counter-productive to say that if, in fact, they were trying to manufacture a compelling story for their readers. In light of their culture, it would have been incredibly illogical and counterintuitive to use that detail if they were simply making the whole thing up.

Truly, the gospel writers didn't make up the story of the resurrection. They never would have written the story the way they did unless, of course, it actually happened that way.

Giving An Account For Your Hope

For much more on this topic, I would strongly encourage you to read *Reason for God* by Tim Keller. Within the book is an entire chapter specifically devoted to defending the resurrection of Christ. There are other great books on this subject as well, such as *Case for Christ* by Lee Strobel. Go check them out.

Reading books like these will not only encourage you personally in your faith, but it will also equip you to "give an account for the hope to which you have been called" as you boldly share your faith with others (1 Pt. 3:15).

When doubt comes on you like a stormy gale,

Lay down your anchor in the resurrection and behind the veil.

Up to this point, we have stressed the importance of how to deal with different viewpoints, what to do with competing claims, and why the resurrection gives us an anchor of confidence in the raging storms of doubt. The first five pointers were more *intellectual* pointers because they largely concerned the *mind*. But the next five pointers will be more *practical* pointers because they largely focus on the *heart*—one's personal, emotional, and psychological well-being. As such, the final pointers will share some practical steps for how you can best thrive in college as a Christian on a day-to-day basis.

PART 2

COMMUNITY, CONFORMITY, IDENTITY... AND THE HEART OF THE CHRISTIAN COLLEGE STUDENT

PLUG IN TO A CHRISTIAN COMMUNITY

Two are better than one... For if they fall, one will lift up his fellow.
But woe to him who is alone when he falls and has not another to lift
him up! And though a man might prevail against one who is alone,
two will withstand him—a threefold cord is not quickly broken.
- Ecclesiastes 4:9-12

We're well into the digital age, so I think it's safe to assume that a large majority of us have smart phones. For most of us—and maybe to a fault—our devices have become a seamless extension of ourselves. It's the first thing we check once we wake up in the morning. It's the last thing we check before we turn in for the night. And it's the heartbeat of our clicking, checking, and sending all throughout the day in between. In fact, studies have shown that the average person checks their device 85 *times per day*.[17]

Don't get me wrong; the smart phone is an extremely helpful and efficient form of communication. However, despite all the advantages it offers, it has one glaring precondition: it must be charged in order to function, and then recharged periodically.

It's a terrible thing possessing a dead phone and having no way to recharge it. We've all been there. But the cruel reality is that your phone will eventually hit 0% without a charge. It needs a steady surge of electricity in order to function.

And our walk with God works in a similar way as well. The vitality of our faith cannot last indefinitely without the certain, periodic charge of Christian community. No matter who you are, without this frequent charge, your faith will eventually flat line.

For your utmost wellbeing and functionality as a Christian, it is essential that you plug in to a core Christian community. This is easily the most important practical tip I can give you. Belong to a core Christian community—not because it will check off an obligation to family or to God, but because *it will be life and vitality to you personally*.

> **It is essential that you plug in to a core Christian community.**

There are a number of reasons why plugging in to Christian community in college is so important. Let's explore five of them.

1. You are weaker than you think.

That might sound pessimistic, but it's actually not. This concept is not just relevant for Christian college students, but for full-time pastors as well. It doesn't matter how long or short you've been a Christian or how strong or weak you are in resisting temptation. Wherever you fall on the faith spectrum—new, old, passionate, lukewarm, strong, or weak—you need community just as much as anybody else. The need for community isn't a matter of the maturity *of* the Christian; it's a matter of necessity *for* the Christian.

Look at the life of plants. A small sapling and a fully-grown tree both need water. Trees do not graduate from water based on growth. And likewise, you do not graduate from community based on maturity.

Even if you are the coolest, most hyped, most respected, Jesus-loving, Satan-stomping youth group kid on the block, you *will* die spiritually in the college environment if you do not surround yourself with an intentional Christian community.

I had many friends who thought, "Oh, *that won't happen to me. I don't need a core Christian community. Besides, Christians can be weird anyways. And I don't want to be identified with hypocrites or fundamentals. I'll be fine. I'll always be a Christian..."*

The need for community isn't a matter of the maturity of the Christian; it's a matter of necessity for the Christian.

As far as the 'weird' and 'hypocritical' part is concerned, you might be right. There are weird and hypocritical Christians out there, just like there are weird and hypocritical people out there in general. But not all people are weird and hypocritical, and not all Christians are weird and hypocritical, either. Which means there *will* be Christians on campus with whom you can personally connect with and respect. You just have to make the effort and find them. They're there.

And as far as 'always being a Christian'—I just wouldn't bank on it, no matter who you are. Your resolve *will* eventually erode to the conditions of life if it is not firmly rooted in the soil of Christian community. I've seen it happen to the best of my Christian friends, and I don't want to see it happen again. We're just too spiritually weak on our own.

2. You are created in the image of a triune, communal God.

God himself exists in Trinity, which means his very nature is communal. And because we were created in his image, that means we were created for community, too.

What's interesting is that in the creation narrative of Genesis 1-2, there was only *one thing* that God said was 'not good' after He had made everything 'good.' It was not the case that He made something 'not good.' Rather, He deemed it 'not good' that one of his 'very good' creations, Adam, was alone (Gen. 2:18). So God created Eve for him, and then told them to multiply and fill the earth abundantly (Gen. 1:28). Community—not isolation—was God's good design. Through the creation account, God essentially tells us that humanity is not truly humanity without community.

I also love what one of my seminary professors once said: "In God's divine humility, He created us so that we must be fulfilled with something in addition to himself: community."[18] In other words, God doesn't take offense when we desire community; in fact, it's quite the opposite. He takes offense when we downplay our need for it.

> *In God's divine humility, He created us so that we must be fulfilled with something in addition to himself: community.*

Ultimately, when our Triune God created us, He programmed the need for community into the hard drive of our souls. Which means, if we don't plug into a Christian community, then we *will* have a system shut down when it comes to our faith. We simply need like-minded and like-hearted friends.

So, plug into a ministry on campus.

Connect with a Bible study in your dorm.

Commit to a church body in your community.

And then invest yourself into them.

If God exists in community (as Father, Son, and Spirit), and if Jesus felt the need to surround himself with a larger community of 12 disciples and a smaller core group of 3 (Peter, James, and John), we would be foolish to think that we can get by without Christian community.

3. You will encounter relational difficulties.

Developing a sense of meaningful community can often be hard, especially in a completely foreign environment such as college. Whether you're an incoming freshman or a struggling junior, forming community can often be difficult.

You'll sometimes feel lonely.

You'll sometimes feel like no one is making an effort with you.

You'll sometimes even feel like making good, close friends is virtually impossible.

But that's not true. It may be awkward trying to jumpstart a sense of community with people you've never met before. But just do it anyways. Lean into that awesome awkwardness. Embrace the weirdness of inviting someone to get lunch with you whom you've only met once. Who knows, it might not go well. Or, you might find a best friend. Just give it a try. Put yourself out on a limb.

What you're probably unaware of is that nearly everyone around you is feeling that same desire for community as well, but they're having an equally hard time going about it.

So be the leader that everyone wants to follow and no one really knows how to be, and reach out; plant seeds of intentionality; endure the loneliness even when it looks like there's nothing 'relational' sprouting to the surface; and toil with the social awkwardness time and time again... but I promise, in the process, you'll reap a harvest of good relationships.

4. Christian community exists as the direct means through which God will minister to you personally.

Too often, we reduce Christian community to nothing more than attending and participating. But it's so much more than that. One thing we seem to forget is that God established his church—Christian community—to be the direct means through which He will minister to you and to others. He has given each member of the church different spiritual gifts for the purpose of ministering to one another and advancing the kingdom (1 Co. 12). If a Christian had every spiritual gift, then they would be self-sufficient and would not need to depend on anyone else. That person wouldn't need Christian community. But God gives each of us *few* gifts so that we will learn to depend on one another in our weaknesses and serve one another with our strengths.

The beauty of the Christian community is that God will use you to minister to others, and He will use others to minister to you. Therefore, if you cut yourself off from Christian community, you are not only cutting yourself off from the ways that God is trying to minister to you through others, but you are also cutting yourself off from

The beauty of the Christian community is that God will use you to minister to others, and He will use others to minister to you.

the ways that God is trying to minister to others through you.

So don't shortchange your wellbeing by not allowing others into *your* life. And don't shortchange others' wellbeing by not being involved in *their* life.

The Christian community is God's tangible, physical expression of his grace, provision, and ministry to you personally. Sure, it's made of sinful people, so it will fail you and sin against you from time to time. But if this community was perfect, then Jesus would not have had to die to save it. Which means you shouldn't 'die' to this community because of one, two, or even three bad experiences. Stick around. They need your grace as much as you need their community.

5. You get to know God better through community than through isolation.

Another advantage to plugging into a Christian community is that you will get to know God *more accurately* and *more fully* through the context of community than all by yourself.

This concept shouldn't seem too unusual. If you think about it, you get to know your friends more accurately and more fully through the context of community—than just all by yourself—as well. To be sure, there will be some elements of your friend's personality that you will only get to know through a one-on-one setting with them; but at the same time, there will be other elements of their personality that can only be brought out in the context of larger groups. Which means you won't get to know them that well if you only see them in one, limited context. If you want to get to know their *full* personality, you would need to observe them in both personal and public settings. (This is also a good tip for dating, FYI).

CS Lewis described this concept quite profoundly in his book, *The Four Loves*, as he pondered some of his closest friendships in life. Lewis was part of a famous circle of three friends called 'The Inklings,' which included J.R.R. Tolkien, the author of *The Lord of the Rings*, and another author, Charles Williams, who unexpectedly died after World War II.[19] Here's what Lewis had to say:

> In each of my friends there is something that only some other friend can fully bring out. By myself I am not large enough to call the whole man into activity; I want other lights than my own to show all his facets. Now that Charles [Williams] is dead, I shall never again see Ronald's [Tolkien's] reaction to a specifically Charles joke. Far from having more of Ronald, having him 'to myself' now that Charles is away, I have less of Ronald . . . In this, Friendship exhibits a glorious "nearness by resemblance" to heaven itself where the very multitude of the blessed (which no man can number) increases the fruition which each of us has of God. For every soul, seeing Him in her own way, doubtless communicates that unique vision to all the rest.[20]

In other words, the interactions among the three friends brought out the fullest personalities of each individual person. When the three were together, they were able to see the full range of each person's personality. But when only two of the friends were together—without the third friend— the friendship between the two suffered also. When Charles died, two things happened: 1) Tolkien was not able to see the part of Lewis' personality that only Charles could bring out, and likewise, 2) Lewis was not able to see the part of Tolkien's personality that only Charles could bring out.

And the principle applies all the way around—one person cannot bring out the full personality of another in the same way that a community can. Ultimately, Lewis is saying that it takes a community to truly know an individual.[21]

The same can be said for how we come to know God as well. The Christian community shines the

> **It takes a community to truly know an individual.**

light of their unique callings and experiences on different facets of God's character, and it's through that larger framework that we get to know God in deeper and more glorious ways. Truly, when we're in community, we are enabled to know God better than we would be able to all by ourselves.

Shameless Plug

My shameless plug is that you need to plug into a Christian community. Because if you don't, it will be a shame in more ways than one. You need to plug into a Christian community because it will be a surge of vitality to your otherwise depleting sense of faith and a source of vibrancy to the overall quality of your relationships.

When you look back on your college experience, you probably will not remember a certain lesson in Bible study or a particular sermon point from a campus ministry night. But what you *will* remember will be the people you met, the community you formed, and the memories you shared with them—and how those things held you up spiritually, whether you realized it at the time or not.

God promises us that if we pray anything according to his will, then

He will not only hear our prayer, but will also answer our prayer (Jn. 15:7; 1 Jn. 5:14). It's certainly God's will that you connect with a core group of Christian friends, so pray that He will provide it for you. Don't wait *passively* for him to come through by sitting in your dorm room twiddling your thumbs. Rather, wait *proactively* for him to come through by visiting ministries, inviting people to share meals with you, and sowing seeds of intentionality. And when that's all said and done, praise him when He answers your prayer... *because He's promised to.*

Whatever you do, plug yourself into a core Christian community.

But in terms of community, don't *only* do that, either.

That leads to the next pointer.

SEEK CHRISTIAN COMMUNITY, BUT DO NOT ONLY SEEK CHRISTIAN COMMUNITY

We are ambassadors for Christ, God making his appeal through
us. We implore you on behalf of Christ, be reconciled to God.
-2 Corinthians 5:20

In our day and age, dieting has become an especially trendy topic. All the new technological advancements in health sciences and nutrition research have provided us a window for seeing the variety of ways our bodies process different foods. As a result, many dieting plans have been created and even custom-tailored to fit your health needs. I don't think there have been more categories for dieting and losing weight than there are currently in our culture.

However, even though there are thousands of different diets to choose from, all diets essentially have two main things in common: 1) an emphasis of a core food group and 2) a connection to peripheral food groups. In other words, while diets are *defined* by a core food group, they're not *limited* to that core food group, either.

Take a vegetarian diet, for example. If you are a vegetarian, that means your diet is defined by the core food group of vegetables, but it doesn't mean your diet only consists of vegetables, either. You probably eat a variety of nuts, fruits, and breads as well. In fact, it's healthier to partake in multiple food groups than to only eat from one food group anyways—because your body needs other minerals and proteins in order to function.

In a similar way, dieting can serve as a helpful metaphor for how we are to approach our relationships as Christians, too. Our community should center on a core group of Christians, but it shouldn't be limited to only Christians, either. We should have friends who are religiously and culturally different than we are. In fact, it's healthier to have a diverse community than to only have Christian friends anyways—because our faith needs more than just Christian friends in order to thrive.

> *Our community should center on a core group of Christians, but it shouldn't be limited to only Christians, either.*

It's actually unbiblical to only have Christian friends. God calls us to reach out and to build community with all types of people, and Jesus' lifestyle was a perfect example of that calling.

> *Our faith needs more than just Christian friends in order to thrive.*

Jesus' community consisted of a core group of disciples, but his community wasn't limited to his only disciples, either. Jesus befriended all people: He challenged the religious elite and befriended the religious outcast; He showed compassion on the rich and comforted the poor; He shared lunch with Jews and dinner with Gentiles; He reasoned with political activists and listened to political pacifists. He reached up to the high class of society, and he reached down to the low class of society. Color of skin, background of class, perspective of religion—these cultural lines did not so much *divide* his type of community so much as they *defined* the extensiveness of his community.

Christ's arms were open to all people, and as Christ-followers, ours should be as well—especially since college hosts a considerably diverse community. In this chapter, I want to emphasize several things: 1) describe the community culture you can typically expect in college, 2) explain how Christians should make community, and 3) give some practical tips that can help mold your community after the model of Jesus.

The Community Culture of College

In terms of a community culture, the college campus is unlike any other that you will ever experience in the rest of your life. It is a tight-knit community woven with *hundreds* of threads of perspectives, religions, ethnicities, and backgrounds. In college, you will meet people who are high-class, low-class, middle-class; black, white, brown, yellow; Libertarian, Republican, Democrat; public-schooled, private-schooled, home-schooled; Evangelical, Catholic, Muslim, Buddhist, Hindu, Atheist— and nearly any combination of any of those factors.

The culture is about as diverse as the assortment of buffet choices at Golden Corral. Only at Golden Corral is it possible to have lamb chops, pancakes, carrots, cereal, and gummy bears—all on one platter. And only in college is it possible to have a Muslim, a Libertarian, a home-schooler, a Buddhist, a Democrat, a private-schooler, an Indian, an Evangelical, an Asian, and an Atheist—all in one class. Truly, college is a cultural buffet of diversity. Whatever type of person you'd like to meet, whatever type of perspective you'd like to hear—you'll likely be able to.

One of the reasons the university culture is so special is precisely because *within a one-mile radius, you have access to virtually every type of person on earth who is your age.* That's simply incredible. Don't take this for granted. You probably will not be around such diversity ever again in your life.

The college campus is essentially a one-mile radius where you have access to virtually every type of person on earth who is your age.

Personally, I distinctly remember one of my leadership classes where each student had to tell the class where he/she fell on the religious spectrum and what their faith (or lack thereof) meant to them. I took note of people's responses, and the results were astonishing. In that one class there were 5 Evangelical Christians, 4 Catholics, 1 Hindu-Buddhist, 1 Jew, 1 Muslim, 1 pantheist, 5 agnostics, and 2 atheists.

Now, that might seem like an extreme example of religious diversity, but I don't think it's too far off from the secular classroom demographic. So I wouldn't expect anything less for what you might experience yourself.

This means you will have an incredible opportunity to do several things that you might not get the chance to do again (at least to this degree):

- Meet a diverse group of amazing people,
- Sharpen your own perspectives, and
- Be a strategic influence for the gospel.

The Bible tells you to go to the nations to share the gospel... but in college, the nations come to you. That's pretty awesome.

As a Christian, your categorical presence might feel considerably small in the classroom, but if you take a stand, your gospel presence will be largely felt by your peers. Statistics show that our presence as Christians is becoming increasingly smaller, but that only means our opportunity for gospel impact is becoming increasingly larger as well.

As they say, light often shines brightest in the darkest of environments. As a Christian in a vastly non-Christian college culture, take heart—you've been blessed with a unique opportunity to shine the light of Christ to an area in our culture that might as well be considered one of the darkest, most unreached mission fields there is.

The college campus may be one of the darkest, most unreached missions fields there is.

Therefore, reach out to your classmates, your suitemates, and your fraternity brothers or sorority sisters—you'll never know where they are spiritually unless you take interest in them and befriend them. Invite them to lunch, ask good questions, be a blessing to them, and share your faith with gentleness, sincerity, and confidence. More often than not, you'll be surprised by how interested your friends are to hear what you have to say about Jesus.

So build community with people who are not like you, and develop relationships with all types of people—just as Jesus did.

But even though that's important, it can still be rather difficult. In fact, for most Christians, there's *one* pattern of community development that often prevents them from forming meaningful, intentional relationships with non-Christians. And it's infamously known as the 'Christian Huddle.'

The 'Huddle-Based' Christian Community

As we established in the last chapter, it's important to seek a core Christian community by plugging into a campus ministry and/or local church. You certainly need it. However, I do have one forewarning: Once you *do* find that core Christian community, you will face the immediate temptation to feel comfortable and complacent with only that community.

It'll be extremely easy to think, "*Alright, my community needs are met. I don't feel the need to pursue any more community now.*" Whether you consciously think that or not, the end result will be the same—you will lose the desire to pursue community with non-Christians. But when that happens, your Christian community—which is a great thing—will reduce to nothing more than a 'Christian Huddle.'

The Bible tells you to go to the nations to share the gospel... but in college, the nations come to you.

What do I mean by that? Think about a football game for a minute. Before the offense carries out their play of choice, all the players gather tightly together and form a huddle. They're all face-to-face, shoulder-to-shoulder, and arm-over-arm. Everyone turns their focus to the inside of the huddle, and as a result, turns their back to everyone else outside of the huddle.

That's exactly what the 'Christian Huddle' looks like. It happens when Christians do everything together. They group together and stay grouped together. In the cafeteria, they only eat with Christians. In the dorms, they only live with Christians. In the classroom, they only sit with Christians. They're great at engaging with one another, but they're not so great at engaging with anyone else.

Don't get me wrong, having awesome Christian friends is certainly a blessing. Satan hates it when you get plugged into a core Christian community. But, if Satan can get you to stay in that community only—he's still won half the fight.

How so? Because when Christians stay huddled-up, we give Satan the image that he wants to convey to the world about us anyways: that we're a bunch of butts. See, when outsider, non-Christians look upon this 'huddle,' all they can see is *a group of buttocks in every direction*. Let's not help Satan acquire that image of us by constantly huddling up.

So, if our community shouldn't look like a 'huddle', then what should it look like?

The 'Team-Based' Christian Community

Instead of your community looking like a huddle, God desires for your community to look more like a *team* instead. It's certainly necessary for a football team to huddle-up as a core, but it does not stay that way. Rather, it breaks into formation and then carries out an action. It is a collective movement of different individuals working together towards a common goal—one that often huddles, but more often plays their roles.

In the same way, that's how we should approach our community as Christians. We are to be a collective movement of different individuals working together towards a common goal—one that often huddles at church, in campus ministries, or in small groups, but more often engages the community around us. We certainly need to come together frequently as a core, but we should not stay that way. Rather, we need to break into our relative positions of life—whether that is a fraternity, major, intramural team, or dormitory suite—and play an active role in the position that God has placed us in to the best of our ability.

When Christians break out of the 'Christian Huddle' community, the outside world no longer sees our buttocks, but our hearts. They don't see us turning our backs on them. They see us opening our arms to them. They don't see us isolating and ignoring. They see us reaching out and engaging. We're not supposed to be huddled up, but spread out.

> *When Jesus called Christians the 'salt of the world,' he was making an analogy: Salt effectively flavors when spread out, not lumped together.*

In fact, that's essentially what Jesus was communicating when he called us the 'salt of the world' (Matt. 5:13). When Jesus called Christians the 'salt of the world,' he was making an analogy: Salt effectively flavors when spread out, not lumped together. When salt is lumped together, it not only tastes disgusting, but it also doesn't fulfill its intended purpose of bringing out the flavor of the food around it. Likewise, when we huddle in our groups and refuse to go out into the world, we not only become a bad taste to the world's taste buds, but we also fail to bring the flavor of Christ to the communities we've been placed in.

> *Huddle up with other believers periodically, but break out of it regularly.*

Therefore, resist the temptation to participate in the 'Christian Huddle.' It's stagnant, distasteful, and ineffective. Strive instead to develop a sense of community that's like a team. Yes, huddle up with other believers periodically, but break out of it regularly. Strategically position yourself into non-Christian communities that can be found all around campus.

"But how can I do that?"

Practically, there are many, many ways for you to avoid the pitfalls of an only-Christian community and to form meaningful relationships with others. For example...

- Form an intramural team with people in your dorm.
- Join a fraternity or sorority.
- Participate in different clubs, like philanthropy or business.
- Host a dorm meal and make pancakes or cookies for people walking by. (I promise, they will not easily forget you for that.)
- Sit with random people in the cafeteria and make new friends.
- Organize weekly study groups with several of your non-believing classmates.
- Visit other religious student groups, such as the Muslim Student Association or the Hillel Group.
- Get a job on campus that allows you to work directly with your fellow student body (i.e. working in the ticket office, being a Resident Advisor, or serving coffee at everyone's favorite coffee shop).

Overall, there are hundreds of opportunities to mold your community after the model of Jesus' community—and to not get caught up in the 'Christian Huddle.'

One thing my roommates and I did to expand our community on campus was to purchase a meal plan for all four years of college. If you can afford a meal plan, I would highly encourage you to get one. It's worth it, because meal times represent much more than just meal times, but community time. Just think about it: most of your meals are spent with the people you are the closest with. At the lunch table, you'll naturally sit with your best friends. If you're going on a date, you'll probably go out for a meal. For us, purchasing a meal plan was our strategic way of getting to know people on campus who we wouldn't get the opportunity to know otherwise. Our meal plan was our ticket to meeting new people, having meaningful conversations, and developing a community outside of our core Christian one.

But for you, your way to build a broad community might not be purchasing a meal plan, but joining a fraternity or sorority, investing in a social group, or working at the student center. Whatever you choose to do, the ultimate goal is the same: Get to know non-Christians who are like you and who are not like you. Become genuine friends with them. Share the gospel with them. Don't treat them as evangelistic projects. *Understand that they are images of God who are able to add unique forms of value, wisdom, and inspiration into your life that other Christians cannot.* And simply delight in your unique friendship you have with them. There are many, many ways to be missional. Pick one or two and expand your community.

The truth is, if you only have Christian friends, you will surely shortchange the quality of your community and the quality of your college experience. If your community is narrow, your joy will be narrow. But if your community is broad and multi-dimensional, so also will be your joy.

> **If you only have Christian friends, you will surely shortchange the quality of your community and the quality of your college experience.**

Still, you might ask, *"How can I have both non-Christian friends and Christian friends without putting myself in compromising situations? I don't want it to look like I'm riding the fence!"* That's a great objection, and that segues right into the next pointer.

POINTER #8
DON'T RIDE THE FENCE

Elijah came near to all the people and said, "How long will you go limping between two different opinions? If the LORD is God, follow him; but if Baal, then follow him."
–1 Kings 18:21

"Choose this day whom you will serve"
–Joshua 24:15

The saying, 'riding the fence' is a common idiom we use for explaining our desire to do two different things at the same time... but never fully being able to do either. It's a popular phrase, but not exactly a positive one.

Try to gather a mental image of what it looks like to 'ride the fence': one leg is on one side of the fence, and the other leg is on the other side of the fence... which means (if you're a guy) that your most vulnerable area has now become even more vulnerable, and you're probably going to get hurt... *hurt bad.*

Think, 'America's Funniest Home Videos' or 'YouTube Fail Playlist' where a guy's skateboard snaps in half as he is grinding down a pipe, and he painfully catches it between his legs; or where a gymnast loses his footing and splits the balance beam in an unlucky way; or where someone tries to hop a fence and, to his utter dismay, gets caught right in the middle of his stride.

We laugh, but only because it didn't happen to us. No doubt, these are very painful, unfortunate experiences. But each scene illustrates an important principle: when your feet are positioned on different sides of the same boundary, *you're going to get hurt.*

In the same way, 'riding the fence' is no different when it comes to your faith. But what exactly does it mean to 'ride the fence' with your faith, especially at the collegiate level?

Generally, 'riding the fence' mainly concerns how your convictions and community play out. It mostly happens when, on one hand, you want to uphold your Christian convictions, but on the other hand, you want to be accepted by a non-Christian community. Your moral integrity and your social acceptance can often feel like they're constantly at odds, or it can feel like a dangerous balancing act that puts you right on the fence.

But it doesn't have to be that way.

It can certainly be a struggle figuring out how to navigate wisely through these two circles. But as we'll see, 'riding the fence' is not so much a matter of the *community you share* so much as it is a matter of the *convictions you hold.*

We often equate 'community' to be the 'different sides of the fence' (such as a Christian community on one side and a non-Christian community on the other side) and 'convictions' to be the 'fence' itself, or our ethical boundaries. It's natural to

> *'Riding the fence' is not so much a matter of the community you share so much as it is a matter of the convictions you hold.*

feel like we must 'ride the fence' of our convictions in order to truly share community with both groups. But ultimately, this is a false dilemma. Let me explain why by giving a practical reason and then a theological reason.

The False Dilemma

Practically, as we discussed in the past two chapters, it's true that you need a core group of Christian friends, and it's also true that you are called to pursue a diverse community just like Jesus did. But that doesn't mean your convictions have to be influenced by each group of communities, either. Think of your core group of Christian friends as your *intimate* community—whom you seek to be influenced by—and your broader community as your *intentional* community—whom you seek to influence.

Many Christians entering college feel like there is an inherent tension in sharing community with both Christian and non-Christian friend groups. They think, "*If I really want to have community with my fraternity brothers, then I will have to do X.*" And, "*If I really want to be accepted by my campus ministry friends, then I will have to do Y.*" And so, they feel the need to adjust their convictions from time to time in order to be truly accepted into both communities. It's tempting to think your convictions must be influenced by each group in order to have true community with each group.

But that's a false dilemma because it's built on a false assumption, namely, that you can only have community with people so long as your lifestyle is in alignment with theirs, or that they will only accept you as long as you are exactly like them. But that's not true.

The reality is, when you are in a non-Christian community—and you stick to your Christian convictions—what you can generally expect is not alienation, but admiration. Let that sink in. So long as you're not

> *When you are in a non-Christian community—and you stick to your Christian convictions—what you can generally expect is not alienation, but admiration.*

domineering or judgmental, you can expect to be welcomed in a unique way. Sure, there might be some people who reject you or even mock you for your faith. But in most cases, the opposite seems to hold true.

Personally, when I hung out with my non-Christian friends and chose not to drink under-age, smoke weed, or do anything inappropriate with the opposite sex—they weren't bewildered by my convictions as much as they were bewildered that I still wanted to be a part of their community. What I thought would turn them off to me was actually a breath of fresh air to them. When I stuck to my convictions, they became convinced that I didn't hang around them because of what they did or didn't do as an activity, but because I was genuinely interested in them as people. Even though I didn't condone what they did, they felt loved as people regardless—so they readily welcomed me, with my Christian convictions and all.

Likewise, if you stick to your Christian principles, you might find a greater sense of acceptance from this crowd than if you just went along with the crowd. To them, you might stick out in an attractive, appealing way—one that shows them their value, and one that points them to Christ. Most importantly, they'll be able to witness first-hand someone who actually lives out their beliefs, which is a big deal. It's absolutely possible to be relatable, down-to-earth, and likable without being worldly.

Forming meaningful non-Christian community while upholding Christian convictions is certainly not a dilemma *practically*. But it's also not a dilemma *theologically*.

The gospel tells us that there is no fundamental difference between Christians and non-Christians insofar as our humanity is concerned. It says all people are equally sinful, all people are equally in need of a Savior, and all people are equally offered a Savior in Christ (Rom. 3:23). Which means you are no different, no better, and no worse than anyone else. It cancels everyone's pride and humbles everyone's spirit. This means we are able to relate with anyone at the most fundamental level—one that goes beyond class, background, morality, or lifestyle.

In order to have a relationship with anyone, you must first establish a commonality. And the gospel does exactly that by helping you see a fundamental, inherent commonality between all people. Its

The gospel declares that all people are equally sinful, all people are equally in need of a Savior, and all people are equally offered a Savior in Christ.

commonality is not about what school you go to, what dormitory you live in, or what major you are pursuing. It's much deeper than that: it's about who we are as people. The gospel gives us the most compelling reason for why we can connect with anyone.

Therefore, it's wrong to think that we can only have community with people until we adjust our convictions. On the contrary, it's precisely these gospel-convictions that *empower* us to form community with all types of people.

It's All About Acceptance

The real issue of 'riding the fence', it seems, generally has to do with seeking acceptance and approval from others. Wanting community with others and acceptance from others is not a bad thing. However, when securing people's acceptance becomes the most important thing to you, it can become a dangerous thing. This is because you will sacrifice anything—especially your convictions—in order to get it. You will begin to conform your convictions to get community, and the results will be catastrophic.

Scripture is loaded with stories and forewarnings about 'riding the fence' in this way. You see a prime example of this in Galatians 2, where the Apostle Paul called out Peter for riding the fence with his convictions and community. As the text indicates, Peter enjoyed community with the Gentiles and the Jews—*but not at the same time.*

Around the Gentiles, he acted one way. But around the Jews, he acted another way. On the surface, it looked like an issue of his community, but underneath, it was more of an issue of his convictions (Gal. 2:11-14). Peter's faith essentially resembled a chameleon. He changed the colors of his convictions in order to blend in with certain social groups. When he was with the Gentiles, his convictions were bright green. But when he was with the Jews, his convictions were blood red.

And so, the Apostle Paul reprimanded Peter for 'riding the fence' with his convictions, changing them according to what community was around him at the time—and not on Christ. Peter's issue was not that he had multiple, contrasting communities, but that he had multiple, contrasting convictions in those communities. By the 'riding the fence,' Peter forfeited his witness and counterfeited his relationships.

There's nothing wrong with having multiple, contrasting communities; the issue is having multiple, contrasting convictions in those communities.

What About You?

Like Peter, many Christians will end up making compromises in their faith that they think will secure people's acceptance, whether it actually does so or not.

One of the most ridiculous conversations I had in college revolved around this very topic. I vividly remember talking with this guy who said he was most effective as a 'witness for Christ' when he was hammered drunk. He explained that when he was drunk, he was best able to relate to his non-Christian peers and share Christ without inhibitions. He argued that he gained more credibility with his non-Christian friends when he was *more* like them (plastered) than when he was *less* like them (sober). True story. In one sense, he was trying to be a part of the Christian community; in another sense, he was trying to be a part of the non-Christian community. But his methods didn't exactly translate successfully. He wanted to be a Christian witness and he wanted others' acceptance, but compromising his faith didn't really help either case.

That's an extreme example, but we can easily do this same type of thing in a variety of ways. Maybe it's cussing in order to fit in. Maybe it's dating a non-Christian in order to feel approved. Maybe it's exaggerating in order to score people's approval. Maybe it's dressing in a way that wouldn't make your Ma or Pa or Jesus proud in order to catch the eyes of that certain someone. Or maybe it's drinking underage in order to fit in.

The main question becomes, when we compromise our faith, are we gaining more community in the process, or are we actually losing it?

It's natural to assume that if we 'ride the fence' of our convictions for acceptance into both Christian and non-Christian communities, then we'll gain more community in the process. But in reality, the opposite is actually true. Here's why.

Bending Your Convictions = Fabricating Your Community

When you 'ride the fence' of your convictions in favor of community, you will not only lose your convictions, but *you'll actually lose a true sense of community, too.*

If you are in a non-Christian circle and acceptance is your main concern, then you might suspend your Christian convictions because the acceptance of others is more important to you at the moment than what you believe. And if you are in a Christian circle and acceptance is your main concern, then you might adhere to your Christian convictions because acceptance of others is more important to you at the moment than what you actually believe. In other words, conviction takes a back seat to community.

What's ironic, however, is that it might appear like you are gaining community by adapting your convictions because you're appealing to both types of communities. But the reality is that you are actually not connecting at all. Instead, it's a projection of yourself into each of those circles that's getting affirmed and accepted—*not the real you.*

Think back to Peter. He was one person to the Gentiles, and he was another person to the Jews. And the result is that neither the Gentiles nor Jews really accepted the *real* Peter; they only accepted the type of Peter that was being projected into their circle.

Likewise, if you fabricate a 'Christian' version of yourself for acceptance into Christian circles, and if you fabricate a 'non-Christian' version of your-self for acceptance into non-Christian circles, the result is a fabricated sense of acceptance on either side of the fence. The real you is stuck in the middle of the fence, not feeling known or loved by either side.

That's a miserable place to be. If you 'ride the fence' with your convic-tions, you will not only forfeit your convictions, but you will also coun-terfeit your community. But thank-fully, it doesn't have to be that way.

> *If you 'ride the fence' with your convictions, you will forfeit your witness and counterfeit your relationships.*

Upholding Your Convictions = Gaining True Community

Alternatively, when you do not 'ride the fence' in favor of community, you will not only keep your convictions, but *you'll actually gain a truer sense of community, too.*

If you are in a non-Christian circle and following Christ is your main concern, then you will stick to your convictions because that's more impor-tant to you than the acceptance of others. And if you are in a Christian circle and following Christ is your main concern, then you will stick to your convictions because that's more important to you than acceptance, too. In this sense, acceptance takes a back seat to convictions.

It's natural to think that you would be sacrificing a larger sense of com-munity by sticking to your convictions. But ironically, the reality is that you will actually be gaining a more authentic community and connecting a lot better after all. Why? Because both groups will know you based on who you really are, not who you are trying to be for them. It's no longer the projection of yourself into each community that's getting affirmed and accepted—it's *the real you*. And as a result, the genuineness of your community increases, not decreases.

> *If you don't 'ride the fence' with your convictions, you'll actually gain a truer sense of both your convictions and community.*

Truly, if you 'ride the fence' with your convictions, you'll lose both your convictions and your community. But if you don't 'ride the fence,' you'll actually gain a truer sense of both.

Jump In With Two Feet

I've heard it said that if you live with one foot in Christianity and with one foot in the world, then you will be miserable in both. But if you live with two feet in either one, life will be much better for you. You'll save yourself a lot of inauthenticity, exhaustion, and hurt if you choose to jump in with both feet.

> *If you live with one foot in Christianity and with one foot in the world, then you will be miserable in both.*

Therefore, Christians, jump into your faith with two feet. Don't divide your interests. You'll get half the delight, half the authenticity, half the quality of relationships, and half the joy of following Christ. Don't short-change yourself. Do yourself a favor, get off the fence, and jump in wholeheartedly.

And here's the catch: when you jump into your faith with both feet, you'll quickly realize that an authentic faith does not look like riding the fence with your convictions, but being a bridge with your community. You can genuinely share community with both Christian and non-Christian communities, just like Jesus. He never stopped holding fast to his convictions, and he never stopped being a bridge between all people and the Father. And as Christians, that's the posture we should joyfully adopt as well.

> *An authentic faith does not look like riding the fence with your convictions, but being a bridge with your community.*

So get off the fence with your convictions and start being a bridge between both the Christian and non-Christian communities.

That's a sure way to make the most of your relationships in college as a Christian.

POINTER #9
DON'T. GO. HOME.

"And my God will supply every need of yours
according to his riches in glory in Christ Jesus."
–Philippians 4:19

Growing up, one of my favorite parts of the summer was going to youth camp.

Just thinking on the words 'youth camp' evokes so many feelings and memories for me.

I think of the deliriously long bus rides. The exhilarating feels of crushing on that cute camper. The throbbing stomach aches from consuming terrible camp food. The putrid stank of a roommate who refused to take a shower for a week. The delightfulness of meeting new people, and the intimacy of connecting more deeply with old friends.

The good and the bad, I loved youth camp. However, it didn't start that way for me.

I can vividly remember hopping on the bus for my first youth camp experience. I wasn't exactly thrilled to go. I didn't know what to expect. And if my parents hadn't forced me, I wouldn't have gone.

Once I got there, the first several days were pretty miserable. I felt out of place. I wasn't having fun. I hardly got sleep because of the rock-solid mattresses and chainsaw snorers in our cabin. The food was sinfully disgusting. I despised camp cheers (I was way too cool for that). And things didn't seem like they were going to get any better, either. I wanted to go home. But of course, that's not how the story ended for me. Eventually, I started connecting with people, making great memories, and feeling at home. In fact, it ended up being such a great experience that I went back every single summer after that.

For many people, the college experience can start off feeling like my first youth camp experience. It's possible to feel more nervous than excited. It's possible to feel out of place, lonely, and uncared for. And you might feel the desire to go home. So what do you do in this case? What's the best decision?

If you're a student, do you throw up the white flag and retreat to the comforts of home? When does push come to shove? And if you're a parent, what does truly loving your college student look like in this time? Does it look like beckoning them to come home or encouraging them to stay put? It's a dilemma that many college students and parents alike struggle with.

As such, this chapter is not only for college students, but for parents of college students as well. I'll begin with an admonition to parents first, and then follow with an encouragement to college students next.

Parents: Hurt vs. Help

Parents, if I can give you one practical tip of parenting your college student, it would be to *not* encourage your child to come home. The first several months of college might be difficult for your child in particular, or the college environment might be difficult for your child in general. I know you love and care for your child, and I know you want to be there for him/her when they are having a hard time in a new place.

However, if you encourage them to come home on the weekends because they are having a hard time connecting with others, you will not be helping them. You will be hurting them and their ability to connect relationally for the long haul.

If you truly want to love them and care for them in this time, then you will prioritize attending to their long-term needs over their short-term inconveniences. What your child really needs in this time of loneliness is not for their loneliness to simply be taken away, but for them to mean-ingfully connect with others. From a parental standpoint, the temptation will be to try to remove the negative issue without actually pushing them towards a positive solution.

Parents, if you truly love your child, then you should prioritize attending to their long-term needs over their short-term inconveniences.

The problem is, even if you are successful in taking the problem away—but you do so without providing a proper solution—then you're not really taking the problem away after all. You're just putting a Band-Aid over it. And what your child really needs in this time, however, is not more Band-Aids to lightly cover over their hurts, but stronger bones to effectively withstand the pressures of life.

So be the great parent that you are and give them the milk of grace and truth. In grace, sympathize with their struggles. And in truth, cater to their needs, not their conveniences. Show them the grace of tender com-passion by entering into their sorrow. But give them the truth of tough love by pointing them unto growth. Doing so will be like a strong dose of spiritual calcium to your child, strengthening the bones of their personal development.

It's true that every momma bird loves her baby chicks. But part of loving them means not allowing them to stay in the nest indefinitely, too. She loves them so much that she wants to see them grow into who they're supposed to be—creatures that fly, not just cry. The momma bird loves her chicks unconditionally; however, the way she demonstrates her love for them changes as her chicks change, appropriate to their stage of life. When the chicks are young, she shows her love *by protecting the nest*. But as the chicks grow older, she shows her love *by sending them out of the nest*.

Imagine a momma bird who didn't allow her chicks to leave the nest. Now, that might be a loving thing to do if her chicks were young and underdeveloped, but it would be an unloving thing to do if they were matured and developed. At that point, she wouldn't helping them, but hurting them. At that point, it wouldn't be love; it would be hate.

Likewise, parents, your child won't learn to grow up if you don't let them truly leave home. I'm sure you want to see them thrive. I'm sure you want to see them love college. I'm sure you want to see them forge life-long friendships and make life-long memories. Then encourage them, yes. Love them, yes. But do not take them out of their social discomforts by beckoning them to come back home. If you do, you will be stunting a very important phase of development for them that may not happen otherwise.

Therefore, commit yourself more to their long-term joy than to their short-term sorrow. Be assured, growth pains hurt—but they're necessary and good. This phase in their social development plays a critical role in shaping them into the kind of adults you want them to be anyways. So, pray for them in their situation. But do not pull them out of their situation.

College Students: House vs. Home

College students, whatever you do, do not go home.

Stay on campus as much as possible.

For those of you who are incoming freshman, this is especially important for you during your first several months of college. This is because your first semester will most likely be the most difficult season in more ways than one. There's a lot of adjusting to do in order to feel at home—which is why it's so tempting to go back home during this time. Instead of struggling to create a new home, it's easy to resort back to the comforts of your old one. But doing so will not solve the issue of loneliness or discomfort; it will just salve the pain temporarily.

And for those of you who have been in college for some time now, the feelings of loneliness or discomfort might not be as a sharp, but that doesn't mean they aren't as relevant. Therefore, the principle is the same: going home might help you avoid the issues, but it will never help you resolve them.

Students, going home might help you avoid struggles with community, but it will never help you resolve them.

Ultimately, if you want to truly develop personally and relationally at the college level, you need to stay on campus and invest yourself into its culture. Whatever year you are, if you stay on campus, you will likely look back and be thankful that you chose to persevere through the difficult seasons of loneliness, awkwardness, or frustration.

Be assured that your perseverance and persistence will go a long way. It might not seem like it in the short-term, but it will always pay dividends in the long-term. If you throw in the towel too early—and decide to go home on the weekends—you might also throw away a prime opportunity of connecting with a great community.

If you don't roll the dice on opportunities to connect with others and instead go home, then you'll never connect with others. But if you choose to roll the dice—and decide to stay on campus during the weekends—you might hit the jackpot, finding some of the best friends you could have ever hoped for.

I can definitely speak from personal experience about this. I went to a university where I didn't know anyone. I'm pretty extraverted, so I didn't have a hard time meeting people; however, I did initially have a hard time creating meaningful relationships. As the opening weeks passed on, the buzz of meeting new people began to wear off and my angst of desiring solid friendships began to set in.

In fact, I distinctly remember one somber, autumn day. I was in my dorm room all by myself, feeling discouraged, downcast, and lonely. My parents came and visited me that day, and I talked to them about my struggle to make meaningful friendships. In our conversation, I debated going home for the weekend, and I even entertained the idea of transferring to another university for the first time. But being the loving parents they are, they encouraged me to stay on campus a couple more weekends and to continue putting myself in a position where I could meet more people.

Quite surprisingly, the following weekend, I spontaneously decided to go camping with a campus ministry and ended up meeting who would be my best friends for the next four years and beyond. It's crazy to think that I had considered going home that very weekend instead. Thankfully, with the encouragement of my parents, I trusted the process of going out on a limb—*just one more time*—and it made all the difference.

Looking back, I often wonder how differently my college experience would have played out had I gone home that weekend instead of going on that camping trip. I might not have met the guys I now consider my best friends. I might have endured a longer season of loneliness. I might have even transferred to another university. Who knows what the outcome could have been.

Whoever you are—whether you're going to college or already in college—I encourage you to stay on campus, invest yourself into its culture, and go out on a limb. Whatever your situation might be, the principle remains the same: if you don't take chances, your situation will not change. But if you do take chances, your situation will be positioned for positive changes to take place.

If you don't take chances, your situation will not change. But if you do take chances, your situation will be positioned for positive changes to take place.

The Harvest Will Come

Parents and college students, as we discussed in under Pointer #6, pray for God to provide community. He promises us that He will answer anything according to His will (Jn. 15:7; 1 Jn. 5:14). And because He desires you to have meaningful Christian community, pray for it, because He wants to answer it.

However, as you are waiting for God to come through and answer your prayer, don't wait *passively*, i.e., sitting in your dorm room and pouting, or driving back home and sulking. Rather, wait *proactively* for God to answer your prayer, i.e., intentionally putting yourself in a position for him to answer your prayer all along, such as staying on campus, visiting campus ministries, going on camping trips, and inviting people to lunch and dinner.

A farmer can't expect the rain to grow his crops if he doesn't first do the hard work of breaking up the land and planting the seeds. In the same way, the college campus is your farming ground. You can't expect God to grow your community if you don't first do the hard work of breaking up your complacency and planting seeds of intentionality.

So put yourself in a position to reap a harvest of community and opportunity. Go out and hoe the land. Go out and plant seeds. Go to a new land and do the same thing. Repeat a couple of times. Pray in faith. But be sure: the rain of God's provision will come pouring down from heaven, nourishing your efforts of desperation into a harvest of abundance.

The energy you sow into your college experience will often be proportionate to the enjoyment you will reap out of your college experience. Likely, the more invested you are on campus, the more you will find special community and unique opportunity.

> *The more invested you are on campus, the more you will find special community and unique opportunity.*

So parents: prioritize the needs of your child.

And students: pursue the means of your growth.

You can count on God to provide you with the things you need. Do your part and be proactive, trust in God's character to you, and lean on God's promises to provide for you.

Don't go home. Stay on campus.

POINTER #10
LEAN IN TO YOUR IDENTITY IN CHRIST

"For he was looking forward to the city with
foundations, whose architect and builder is God."
-Hebrews 11:10

Saving the best for last, the most important pointer I can give you is to lean in to your identity in Christ.

Identity can be a buzzword these days. It's something we all know we have, but we might not know exactly what it refers to. Identity can be your answer to the seemingly simple question, "Who am I?"

A knee-jerk reaction might be to think that our identity refers to our gender, occupation, background, religious affiliation, political affiliation, or any combination of those things. Or, we might think our identity is in being a student, athlete, musician, or employee. However, it goes much deeper than that.

Your identity essentially refers to where you find your greatest sense of self-worth and significance. It's what you've decided is the foundation of who you are. It's your lowest common denominator that determines how everything else in life adds up. It's the thing you cling to most fervently when everything else is taken away.

What is it that gives you a feeling of self-worth? What would you say is foundational to your sense of significance or happiness? What are the things you *must* have in order to feel important, valuable, or secure?

Some of us find our self-worth in our academic achievements. Others of us find it in the approval of others. And others of us may find it in athletic ability or good looks, a relationship or Instagram followers, comfort or status, or even in a respectable morality. We tend to make these things the proof of our significance.

> *Your identity essentially refers to where you find your greatest sense of self-worth and significance.*

Making good grades, having good looks, being in a relationship, achieving great accomplishments, getting accepted into competitive schools, and being moral people are not bad things. In fact, they are blessings! However, when we depend on those things to give us our self-worth, we will be in for quite a surprise as we go through college, and especially for when we go through life.

In this last chapter, I want to talk about two terms that represent how people try to establish an identity in college and beyond. These two terms are 'foundation' and 'direction,' and how they play out in your life is what will either give you a life-draining sense of self-worth or a life-giving sense of self-worth. I want to show you that it's only in making Christ—and how He feels about you—the foundation of your worth that you will be able to live a life directed by freedom and peace.

Overall, your sense of identity will impact every dimension of your college experience and every facet of your life. Let's take a closer look at how 'foundation' and 'direction' critically shape your identity and self-worth.

Foundation & Direction

First, what do you think of when you hear the word, 'foundation'? You might think about a building or a house, right? Large structures need a sturdy foundation; otherwise, they will threaten to collapse under slight circumstances.

In college, I frequented a house that hosted dance parties, and this house...shall we say... had a very *loose* foundation. It's an old house, and its structure didn't exactly benefit from the collective weight of 200 kids jumping up and down on it every month. In fact, because of its frail and fractured infrastructure, the house has teetered on the status of 'condemned' for quite some time now. Houses have a foundation, and it's the structure that provides stability and resilience.

Your sense of identity will impact every dimension of your college experience and every facet of your life.

As people, we have a foundation as well. And similarly, it's the thing at the very bottom of who we are that gives us a stabilizing feeling of personal significance and self-worth. Our foundation is the thing we rely upon as the 'concretizing force' of our life, such that if we didn't have it, life would seem to fall apart. It's what we fall back on when life rattles us, and it's what we depend on in order to feel valuable and secure.

Your direction, on the other hand, essentially constitutes everything else. Whereas your foundation ultimately concerns what's at the bottom of *who are you*, your direction is ultimately the overflow of *what you do*. It primarily concerns your personal performance and present circumstance. It's what is built upon your foundation, which is evident on the surface of your life. Your direction may involve attending a certain university, becoming a more moral person, pursuing excellence in athletics, involving yourself in a romantic relationship, or setting your hopes towards a specific career path.

Your foundation is about your self-worth and significance.

You direction is about your performance and circumstance.

Foundation + Direction = Identity (?)

There are two main ways your identity can be created.

The mantra of culture says our foundation (who we are, our self-worth, our identity) is completely dependent upon our direction (what we do, what your grades are, what college you're going to, what profession you have, how much money you make, how approved you are, etc.).

It's the notion that personal significance is determined by personal performance. It's the idea that your identity is in your ability, and that your work defines your worth. It's to make what you do as the grounds

The mantra of our culture says that who you are is completely determined by what you do.

for who you are. Culture says that your self-worth rises or falls based on your success or situation. However, in the following pages, we'll see why this type of identity is a dead-end.

Thankfully, the Bible provides us another alternative for how we can find self-worth, and it's one that isn't a dead-end, but a road to life and freedom.

The biblical alternative states that your foundation and direction are not dependent upon one another, but rather, are separate, non-overlapping categories. The Bible resoundingly declares that your significance is *not* based on your performance or circumstance. And we'll see why this type of identity is a road to peace instead.

Naturally, you might object and think, "*Well, why is it wrong if I base my self-worth on what I accomplish, or how moral I am, or the person I'm dating? Those things make me feel good about myself!*"

That's a great thought. It's certainly acceptable to celebrate your achievements, strive for moral uprightness, and cherish your significant other. However, the danger with making your significance dependent upon your performance is that whenever you approach your schooling, work, morality, or relationships—it won't ever *just* be about your schooling, work, morality, or relationships—*it will ultimately be about securing your self-worth.* Which means when you approach anything in life, *your self-worth will always be hanging in the balance of your success, failures, or circumstances that are simply out of your control.* We can all agree that that is a dangerous place to be, and there are several reasons why this type of identity is not a viable way to live.

An Identity Built on the Sand

There are 3 main problems with finding your self-worth in achievement or situation. And in college, these problems become significantly worse, not better.

1. Basing your self-worth on your performance or circumstance will naturally breed comparison, insecurity, and anxiety.

Speaking from personal experience, when I was in high school, my entire self-worth could be found on my personal resume. Top of my class.

Captain of several sports teams. Student government representative. Bible study leader. My significance was based wholly on my performance. I felt like I mattered because of all the things I did. My worth was completely wrapped up in my work. I needed achievement to convince others that I was valuable. In fact, I needed achievement and others' approval to convince *myself* that I was valuable. Those things gave me my sense of identity. They were the pillars of my self-worth.

And that's precisely why going to college actually *hurt* me at first. Why? Because the identity I had so tirelessly built, crafted, and polished all through high school—as a way of proving myself—immediately didn't matter any more. The horrid realization hit me like a brick. No one cared I was top of my class. No one cared I was respected by people from high school. No one cared about my hard work and accomplishments.

Basing your self-worth on your performance or circumstance will naturally breed comparison, insecurity, and anxiety.

I can remember my first day of Organic Chemistry so vividly. To start the class, my professor asked for a raise of hands, "*How many of you were valedictorians or salutatorians in high school?*" No joke, half the class of 300 people raised their hands. What a great intimidation tactic.

To say that I felt small and inadequate would be an understatement. The identity I depended on in high school to feel secure and important no longer allowed me to feel secure and important in college. It was almost like feeling naked in public: all the things I had clothed myself with in high school to feel significant were virtually invisible to the eyes of my peers in college. And so, I felt the immense burden to 'clothe' myself in accomplishments, yet again, so that I could feel like I mattered once more.

However, the thought produced in me a disconcerting feeling: when I compared myself to others in my high school, I felt secure with myself. But what a self-inflating, arrogant thing to believe! And when I compared myself to others in college, I felt insecure and ridden with the anxiety to measure up. But what a self-deflating, despairing thing to believe! And that's the problem of basing your self-worth on things that can be compared. You will become deflated

I felt the immense burden to 'clothe' myself in accomplishments, yet again, so that I could feel like I mattered once more.

with despair when you think you compare *worse* to others, and you will become inflated with self-righteousness when you think you compare *better* to others. Your identity will fluctuate between these two life-draining extremes. You'll be stricken with never-ending impulses of delusional pride and unwarranted insecurity.

Overall, this type of identity fails to provide real security. It's a security based on comparison, which is no security at all. You'll never really feel secure; you'll always feel unsettled. It's no way to live. It will suffocate you with selfishness, envy, and anxiety—but that's not all it will do.

2. Basing your self-worth on your performance or circumstance will always make failures and disappointments worse than they actually are.

Take these following scenarios, for example:

- If your self-worth is based on your athletic abilities, what happens if you get a career-ending injury?
- If your self-worth is based on your academic achievements, what happens if you fail an important test, or get rejected from your dream university, or get denied from the business school?

- If your self-worth is based on your acceptance from others, what happens when you go to a new school and don't have any friends? Will you do anything to get the approval of others?
- If your self-worth is based on status, what happens when you don't get the recognition you think you deserve?
- If your self-worth is based on being a respectable Christian person, what happens when you sin...and other people find out about it? Because that *will* happen eventually.

The problem with basing your identity on academics, athletics, or approval is that a failure in this category becomes much more than just a failure. Why? Because when your identity is tied up in them, a failure doesn't just threaten your grade point average, athletic career, or social status... it *threatens your self-worth*... it *threatens you*.

Basing your self-worth on your performance or circumstance will always make failures and disappointments worse than they actually are.

When I failed my first exam in Organic Chemistry, it hurt so badly because it wasn't just a shot at my grade point average, it was a shot at my significance as a person. It was a wrecking ball to one of the pillars of my foundation.

And it works in the same way with anything else. If you base your self-worth on having a girlfriend or a great job, then a break-up doesn't just mean losing a girlfriend and a layoff doesn't just mean losing a great job—it also means losing your sense of personal importance as well.

Under this type of identity, disappointments are magnified and failures are amplified. They end up meaning so much more than they actually mean. And as a result, it will lead to excessive, unwarranted amounts of fear and anxiety.

Certainly, if the first two issues of a performance-based, circumstance-based identity weren't bad enough, there's another reason it can be so deleterious to the college student as well.

3. When you base your self-worth on your performance, you might end up pursuing a career path that you never should have pursued.

When you depend on your performance—grades, major, or career—to establish your self-worth, you might pursue a career path that does not fit with your abilities, passions, and burdens at all. Rather, you might try to become someone you're not.

"But why would people do that?" you might ask. Because when you base your self-worth on your career, then this 'Pre-Awesome' major or this 'Wealthy Profession Major' will

> *When you base your self-worth on your performance, you might end up pursuing a career path that you never should have pursued.*

appear to promise a better type of self-worth than other majors or career paths. Which means you might end up choosing a path that you're not passionate about or gifted in—all in the desperation of proving yourself.

Many college students will try to be doctors or lawyers or accountants when they have no passion for the field at all. This is because being a doctor, lawyer, or accountant in our culture means status, wealth, intelligence... *self-worth* or *security*. There's certainly nothing wrong with becoming a doctor, lawyer, or accountant. But if your motivation for doing so is more about proving your worth than stewarding your passions, then it can be an incredibly selfish way to 'serve' others with your work. Not to mention, it will be an extremely exhausting, life-draining, and unpleasant way to live as well.

Students intoxicated by the 'my-work-is-my-worth' viewpoint tend to seek a profession that they think will give them higher degrees of significance instead of doing something that God actually created them to do all along. As a result, they end up mutilating their strengths, become disillusioned about their weaknesses, and bleed their God-given abilities and passions dry.

Unfortunately, you see this happen all the time. Problem is, when your worth is your work, you tend to zombie-walk down that dead-end path almost instinctively. Studying to be a doctor—even when you have no passion for medicine—will actually seem like the logical thing to do. It's a shame.

Overall, basing your significance on your performance will not only make you disillusioned, but it will also cause you great exhaustion and frustration in one of the most important areas of your life.

Culture Admits It's No Way To Live

I recently heard about a NY *Times* article that talked about people's insane, obsessive, workaholic habits nowadays—that students and employees everywhere are running themselves into the ground when it comes to their work.

The author was a little sarcastic in his interpretation, generally saying: "Do you think employees and students are really sacrificing their sleep, their health, and their relationships on the altar of work or schooling... because they just *really* love their jobs or because they just *really* love their calculus homework?" The answer to his rhetorical question was admittedly, "No."

Then, why are students killing themselves over every point? Why are employees striving so intensely up the corporate ladder?

The columnist reasoned that it's because there's a bigger type of work going on *underneath* their academic or vocational work—and it's the unending, tireless work of people trying to establish their worth through their work. If they achieve this or that, then they are something. If not, then they are nothing. It's the idea that their significance as a person is enslaved to their success as a student/employee.[22] The result is that universities and work places alike have stopped being beautiful places of culture, and instead, have become personal 'Roman Coliseums' for people to duel, strive, and bleed in the hopes of being validated and proven worthy. And it's making people miserable.

When you live out of an identity based on accomplishment or circumstance, life will be an emotional rollercoaster precisely because you have put your identity on the inevitable rollercoaster of human effort and circumstance. Your worth will rise and fall, go up and down, corkscrew, flip, and turn according to things you can't always control. Truly, this unstable type of self-worth will always be flirting with the proverbial, large red-button button of 'SELF-DESTRUCT.' And that's an extremely dangerous and vulnerable place to be.

The Bible communicates that your significance is not based on your performance or circumstance.

But thankfully, Christians don't have to live this way.

The Bible offers a different paradigm, communicating that your significance is *not* based on your performance or circumstance. It separates the two categories of worth and work, of identity and ability, of foundation and direction—carving out a road to real peace and freedom.

Your direction—schooling, athletics, work, and relationships—was never meant to supply your worth and identity in life. These things are simply meant to bless society, serve others, create culture, enjoy life, and love God. Your direction in life is supposed to be an overflow of what you love to do and what you feel a burden for. Your schooling, athletics, work, and relationships should not be coerced to fulfill your need of finding significance.

The question becomes, *"Then where can you get a self-worth that is not is based on your personal performance or your present circumstance? And how can you have a direction that isn't constantly paying tribute to your foundation?"*

An Identity Built on the Rock

While everything else in the world says your efforts and situation determines your personal significance, only the God of the Bible says otherwise.

I understand that might sound like too simple of an answer. So, because you're a smart college student, let's just be strictly *logical* as we further unpack that idea.

Think about it: if one's self-worth is determined by grades, college, career, status, relationships, looks, morality, and accomplishments, then that means their identity is *unstable* because all those things are subject to human failure and unfortunate circumstance.

If an unstable identity is one that *is* subject to circumstance or human effort, then that means a stable identity is one that is *not* subject to circumstance or human effort. Therefore, the only stable identity possible is one that comes from something that is beyond and not determined by human effort or circumstance. And only in the Bible do we find an identity like that: God's love for us and his gospel of grace to us. It's the one source of self-worth in the universe that is not based on our effort or our circumstances.

In the gospel of Christ, God proudly declares, "*You have ultimate self-worth because I say so, and more clearly than that, I demonstrated it by sending my Son to die in your place and to redeem you! You're worth everything to me! And this is by grace through faith, and not by works so that you cannot boast or fret!*"

If you're a Christian, you have access to a type of self-worth that isn't subject to the inevitable rollercoasters of life. It's a type of significance that isn't earned by your performance or determined by your circumstances. Rather, it's given by grace and it's received by faith. You simply accept it, believe it, and live in light of it on a day-to-day basis.

If God only accepts absolute righteousness (i.e. perfection, holiness), and if you have received Jesus' perfect righteousness by faith, then that means God can only perfectly accept you and fully approve of you. Your identity is in the right standing of Jesus, and it has become the basis for why God can never stop loving and accepting you. And God's feelings don't fluctuate for you based on anything you do or don't do. It's unconditional.

Jesus has secured for you maximal acceptance, unconditional love, and perfect security from the only One whose opinion of you really matters most anyways. And if God thinks that way about you, then it doesn't matter what anyone else—*or even you*—thinks about you. Truly, God offers you a type of

> **Jesus has secured for you maximal acceptance, unconditional love, and perfect security from the only One whose opinion of you really matters most anyways.**

self-worth that is better than one you could ever give to yourself. Being a Christian, therefore, is not so much about what you do *for Christ* so much as it is about living in light of who you are *in Christ*.

Leaning into your identity in Christ essentially means finding your greatest sense of self-worth, validation, significance, security, and satisfaction in God's absolute acceptance and love for you, which was given most fully in the person and work of Jesus Christ. It's an identity built on the Rock, unaffected by the waves of circumstance or human failure.

A Foundation in Christ Redeems Your Direction in Life

A self-worth established on the Rock of God's love for you is invaluable for *what it is to you*, but it is also empowering for *what it does for you*, too. It not only provides you with an unshakable foundation, but it also redeems your direction. Let me explain.

If your value as a person is built on the Rock of God's love and acceptance for you, then that means you can finally have a deep sense of peace in your direction (schooling, athletics, friends, etc.). This is because your direction is no longer being used to supply the void of your self-worth.

And it significantly, it reverses the three problems that happen when you base your self-worth on your performance and circumstance.

1. **Finding your self-worth in Christ will help you to stop comparing yourself to others.**
   If your self-worth is in Christ, then your self-worth will not be determined by how well you think you stack up to others. You will stop being anxious and envious.

2. **Finding your self-worth in Christ will prevent you from magnifying failures and misfortunes.**

   When bad grades, lack of recognition, or missed opportunities come—because they will come—your self-worth will be secure. Will you be disappointed? Sure. But in despair? No. When your value is in Christ, bad grades are just bad grades, and a lack of recognition is just a lack of recognition, an injury is just an injury—not reflections of your significance as a person.

3. **Finding your self-worth in Christ will encourage you to pursue something you're actually passionate about.**

   When Christ's love for you is your source of self-worth, then you won't feel the pressure to hop into a career that may *seem* like it promises self-worth and security, such as being a doctor or lawyer. Because you have worth in Christ, you won't feel the need to prove yourself in the job force. Instead, you'll just pursue what you genuinely enjoy.

Ultimately, a self-worth based on performance and circumstance will *enslave* your self-worth to those things. But a self-worth based on Christ's love for you will *save* your self-worth from those things. Because Christ's love for you is not dependent on those things, your self-worth is finally secured.

And paradoxically, possessing a type of self-worth that is separate from your performance or circumstance actually redeems you to have a healthy sense of performance and circumstance after all. In fact, it changes everything. For example...

- When your self-worth isn't based on people's acceptance of you, you'll actually find that people come to like you more anyways.

Why? Because people have stopped being identity-builders to you, but people whom you can enjoy simply for who they are.

- When your self-worth isn't based on academic success, you'll actually find that you come to love academics more for what it is— simply academics, and not a stepping stool for your own identity. Your identity is no longer enslaved to your grades. Which means there's less pressure and there's less on the line, so it's more enjoyable.

- When your self-worth isn't based on money, you can actually enjoy it, give it away, and sacrifice it for the good of others. Money becomes a tool to bless others, not a barometer of your worth or a foundation for your security.

- When your self-worth isn't based on your career, your work will be more refreshing. You won't be working for your job *and* for your self-worth, which is doubly exhausting. Instead, your work will just be work. Nothing more, nothing less.

When you lean in to your identity in Christ, everything else in life becomes redeemed to what it's supposed to be. Your direction is no longer turned inwardly to validate yourself. Rather, it's turned outwardly to serve and enjoy others.

Let me end with a quick illustration that shows how having a self-worth rooted in Christ—separate from human effort and circumstance— can empower a healthy, free, and peaceful life.

Chariots of Fire

The classic movie, *Chariots of Fire*, is based on a true story that features two Olympic track stars, Eric Liddell and Harold Abrahams. What the movie does so well is that it illustrates the nature of each runner's careers by contrasting their identities—showing how different they are from one another even though they had the same vocation.

The movie portrays Harold Abrahams to be someone whose running career was his source of self-worth. His success on the track is what made him feel important and distinguished—it's what gave him significance. His self-worth rose or fell based on how well he performed.

The movie depicts Eric Liddell, however, to be someone whose running career was *not* his source of self-worth. Rather, his self-worth was separate from his career—and it was based on what God thought about him in Christ. How he performed on the track was just secondary.

There's one scene in particular that I'll never forget.

An interviewer asked Abrahams a pointed question, "*What's on the front of your mind as you approach the starting block?*" And his response was absolutely chilling. He replied, "*As I get on the blocks, right before the gun goes off, there is one thing that goes through my mind. And it's this: '**I have 10 seconds to justify my entire existence.**'*" (Bang).

However, the same question was directed at Liddell, and his response was simply inspiring. In fact, it's the most famous quote of the film. He replied, **"When I run, I just... feel God's pleasure."**[23]

In those two statements you have two completely different approaches to life. Abrahams and Liddell were both Olympic runners. On the exterior, they looked exactly alike. But on the interior, they couldn't be more different.

Abrahams ran because he had to. His running career was essentially a self-salvation project. But Liddell's identity was in Christ. And he ran simply because he loved to.

Who do you think experienced more joy in their career, regardless of their success? Abrahams or Liddell? Liddell did.

This is because Abrahams ran for a foundation, for validation, and for a sense of self-worth—and the pressure of it all *suffocated* his love for running. Sure, he had success... but he was absolutely miserable. Liddell, however, ran from a foundation, from validation, and from a sense of self-worth—and it was *oxygen* in his lungs.

How About You?

Where do you find your self-worth? If it's in anything but Jesus' love for you, it will not only fail you from time-to-time, but it will likely make you miserable for most of the time.

If your worth is in Christ, however, you'll have freedom and joy in life because your worth won't always be hanging in the balance of things you can't control. You won't despair and you won't compare. You can work and love what you do. You won't feel forced into a major. You'll see a burden in your society, and you'll help it. And when the storms of failure or misfortunes come your way, you'll be able to endure them precisely because the Rock of your identity and self-worth won't be going anywhere.

Now What?

Whoever you are reading this, I'm sure you are smart. I'm sure you are talented. I'm sure you are driven. Some of you will be reporting the news, blocking a shot into the stands, marketing an incredible product, or creating the next cutting-edge phone application.

At this stage in adulthood, you're metaphorically stepping up to the starting blocks of life... you're getting set... but before the gun goes off... I want to encourage you. Don't run the race of life in order to gain self-worth. Run because in Christ, you have self-worth. Only that will empower you to run—whatever it is you end up doing—and feel God's pleasure.

Take a beautiful photo and feel God's pleasure.
Dunk a basketball and feel God's pleasure.
Write an article and feel God's pleasure.
Create a phone app and feel God's pleasure.
Put a cast on someone and feel God's pleasure.
Fight injustices and feel God's pleasure.
Teach the next generation and feel God's pleasure.

Get a hold of Christ as your foundation, and then let your direction get a hold of you. Lean in to your identity in Christ, and then follow your natural leanings.

Your self-worth is not your grades. Not your university. Not your friends. Not your earning potential. Not your good looks. Not your

> *Lean in to your identity in Christ, and then follow your natural leanings.*

family. Not your followers on social media. An identity in these things is conditional, circumstantial, and therefore, catastrophic. It will never bring peace—only anxiety, despair, and a false sense of security.

Your identity and self-worth is in Christ and what He has done for you. An identity rooted in God's approval for you in Christ is unconditional, never changing, maximal, and always life-giving. It will always bring peace and freedom.

It will free you from the insecurity of always trying to measure up. It will free you from the anxiety of always trying to prove yourself. It will free you from the captivity of others' opinions. It will free your work from constantly paying tribute to your worth. And it will free you to love, serve, and work from the heart without feeling enslaved to getting it in return.

With an identity in Christ, you will be able to "run and not grow weary" (Is. 40:31). The yoke of your direction will be easy and the burden of your work will be light (Mt. 11:30), precisely because your self-worth has already been paid in full and stamped with "it is finished" (Jn. 19:30).

Your self-worth is secure. Now go live from that solid foundation.

THE POINT OF DIFFERENCE, MAKING AN IMPACT

And I tell you, you are Peter, and on this rock I will build my
church, and the gates of hell shall not prevail against it.
- Matthew 16:18

Before you close this book, there's one last thing that needs to be addressed.

We've looked at 10 different pointers—some intellectual and some practical—in the preceding pages, and I hope they have been helpful, practical, and encouraging for you. However, if these 10 pointers do not lead you to do one very important thing, then they will have been for nothing.

Namely, if these 10 pointers do not inspire you to lead an impactful life, then they will have been a failure to you. These 10 pointers are designed to strap you with confidence and launch you into campus for the purpose of making a difference, leaving a legacy, and putting a dent on your college for Christ. Anything less would be subpar.

At the beginning of the book, I explained that my goal was to help the average Christian feel prepared, equipped, and empowered to face the unique challenges of college. However, feeling prepared, equipped, and empowered only gets you as far as the starting line. It will help you for the race, but it is not the race itself. The most important thing is how you run the race. And that's something only you can do. So I hope you move forward in the college environment with confidence—implementing what you've learned, putting it into action, and making a difference.

The opportunity to impact your campus for Christ is always available.

Whether you're a rising freshman or current senior, the opportunity to impact your campus for Christ is always available. No matter what season you're in, God invites you on his mission and longs to use you for his kingdom.

Take heart by listening to Curtis' story. You might relate to him in more ways than one.

From The Sidelines To The Frontlines

Curtis grew up in the church. He was a great guy. Everyone loved him. He played the drums in youth group and participated in a weekly Bible study. He'd been a Christian since he was 7 years old. Church on Sundays and Christian activities Monday through Saturday were all he knew for the first 18 years of his life.

But once he graduated from high school and entered into college, life quickly took a turn.

Within the first weeks of his university environment, he found himself being pulled by the undercurrent of college's strong temptations and compelling worldviews. Underage drinking. Substance abuse. Fast relationships. Religious skepticism. Before long, he was up to his eyes in a world he had never known.

He stopped going to church.

He didn't pursue a campus ministry.

He cut ties with Christian friends.

It's not that he stopped believing in Christ. And it's not like he stopped calling himself a Christian. He just didn't live it out. He put his faith on the top shelf for the time being while he occupied himself with an alluring culture he had yet experienced.

Two years went by, and he had a lot of 'fun.' But after a while, the 'fun' that seemed so exhilarating and satisfying at first increasingly became more and more dull and dissatisfying over time.

The pleasures of immoral living began to sour.

The parties became boring.

His friendships grew superficial.

By the end of his sophomore year, his lifestyle of running from God eventually dead-ended into a back alley of emptiness, isolation, and sadness.

And it was there where he met God. Or, rather, it was there where God met him.

From that moment, God began softening his heart, pulling him out of sin, and giving him a renewed delight in the things of Christ.

Curtis started going to church again. He began attending a campus Bible study. He started connecting with a great community of Christian guys. And a transformation took place. It's not that he cut ties with unbelieving friends or stopped being intellectually curious; it's just that his approach was completely differ-ent. God was changing his heart.

> *No matter what season you're in, God invites you on his mission and longs to use you for his kingdom.*

And over time, his small steps of faithfulness grew into strides of joy. Everyone could see it, too. He was literally a new creation. Even though he was technically a 'Christian' before college, he would tell you that his faith never truly became real to him until the end of his sophomore year. He would gladly tell you that the following two years were by far the best two years of his college experience, and maybe even the best two years of his life.

By his senior year, he had become one of the main leaders at his university's largest campus ministry, and he graduated leaving a legacy upon the lives of many. And since the end of this sophomore year, his trajectory of following Christ hasn't slowed down, either. In fact, I'm proud to call Curtis one of my closest friends to this day.

Curtis has an awesome testimony. He went from being a Christian in name only to being a Christian who made a name for Christ. He went from the sidelines of faith to the frontlines of mission. Curtis' story, however, is not atypical or unachievable. You can be just as much of an influence on campus as Curtis was, no matter who you are.

He went from being a Christian in name only to being a Christian who made a name for Christ.

The question becomes, in view of Curtis' story, what will it be for you?

"Will you follow Christ in college?
"Are you going to make a difference for God's kingdom?"
"How will you make an impact?"

You only have four, short years. And trust me, they will fly by.

If you're about to take that bold step into college, you have the opportunity to make a difference for Christ right from the start. And if you're currently in college, you have the opportunity to start making a difference today. Even if you've been wayward or feel inadequate, Curtis' life is proof that you are never too far off for God to restore you by his grace and use you by his power.

Wherever you are along this collegiate journey, God desires that you be a good steward who does not need to be ashamed (2 Tim. 2:15), and that you make the best use of your time because the days are evil (Eph. 5:16). Whoever you are, the next step is to walk forward in faithfulness and to steward what God has put in front of you right now.

It won't be easy. There will be temptations. There will be skepticism. There will be unknowns. There will be setbacks. But one of the greatest comforts in Scripture is God's promise to us that when we

> *You are never too far off for God to restore you by his grace and use you by his power.*

walk forward in faithfulness, the gates of hell will not be able to prevail against us (Mt. 16:18).

The Gates Of Hell In College

But what does it mean that the 'gates of hell will not prevail against you'? If you've grown up in church, you've likely heard that verse countless times. Whenever I heard that verse, I always pictured that hell was on the attack, but because I was a Christian, I didn't have to worry. Christ was my defense. I assumed hell was on the offensive, and I was on the defensive.

But I later realized that that's not the image Jesus was communicating in that statement. In fact, Jesus was actually communicating the very opposite. When Jesus said, "The gates of hell will not prevail against you," He was communicating that hell was on the *defensive* and

Christians were on the *offensive*.

Think about the image of a gate. Gates are not offensive weapons. No one uses a gate for attack purposes. Gates are defensive structures. They are designed to keep people out. That's it.

Therefore, when Jesus tells us that the gates of hell will not prevail against us, He is saying that when we strive to make a gospel impact in the places where hell seems to have a hold—such as the college campus—we can be assured that hell will not be able to stop us. The gates won't keep us out. The fire won't burn us up. When you follow Christ, you won't merely avoid getting burned, you'll have the power to put out the flames. Hell won't have power over you; in Christ, you'll have power over hell!

In the first several pages of the book, I explained that my desire was for you to not live on your heels as a Christian in defense, but rather, that you'd live on your toes as a Christian on offense. We'll only be able to do so when we take this great promise of Scripture to heart and let it empower our walk.

> *When you follow Christ, you won't merely avoid getting burned, you'll have the power to put out the flames.*

Christian college students, God desires for you to partner with him in breaking the gates of hell, plundering the investments of hell, and over-turning the schemes of hell on the college campus. In the dormitory. In the cafeteria. In the locker room. In the classroom. He's given you all you need in order to live effectively, confidently, and powerfully as a Christian witness (2 Pe. 1:3). Now is the time to start.

Walking Forward In Confidence

For those of you who are about to start your college career, I'm excited for you. You have four great years ahead of you. It'll be a season of opportunity and growth like none other. Be eager to make a difference. I know God eagerly desires to empower you to do so.

And for those of you who are already in college, I'm confident in you. You have experience, connections, and knowledge that rising freshman do not have, and these

> *He went from the sidelines of faith to the frontlines of mission.*

things can enable you to make a difference in a unique way. Get excited and be strategic. At the same time, however, I realize it's possible that some of you feel discouraged, like you've approached college wrongly or wasted your time at first. But take heart—in God's economy, nothing is ever wasted. He promises to redeem all things in your life and use it for good (Rom. 8:28). He has good plans for you and desires to use you in an impactful way *right now*—not in spite of your shortcomings, but because of them.

College will take you through a dimension of life that you've never experienced before. There will be times of happiness and times of hardship, and everything in between. But whatever you go through, rest in the assurance that God is your Father who loves you and will provide for you every step of the way (Ph. 4:19). Know that in Christ, the fires of skepticism, immorality, and idolatry will not overcome you. In fact, you will overcome through him, because "greater is He that is in you, than he that is in the world" (1 Jn. 4:4).

And as you walk through campus, step-by-step, day-by-day, be confident of this:

We have a God who is real,

A Savior who is ruling,

A Spirit who is active,

A Word that is true,

And a Kingdom-community that will overcome.

In Christ, you have no reason to worry and every reason to rejoice.

You can walk through this collegiate chapter of your life with a confident, impactful faith. Why? Because He'll be with you every step of the way.

"And behold, I am with you always, to the end of the age" (Mt. 28:20)

–Jesus

ENDNOTES

1   *The Summit Journal*, December 2014, Volume 14, Issue 11. Page 15. https://
    www.summit.org/archives/journal/Summit_December_Journal.pdf.

2   John Piper, *Amazing Grace in the Life of William Wilberforce*, 2007. http://www.
    desiringgod.org/books/amazing-grace-in-the-life-of-william-wilberforce.

3   For more information on this weighty subject (and other weighty subjects),
    I would encourage you to check out the website, www.ehrmanproject.com.
    Here, you will find a host of short videos from the world's leading biblical
    scholars that address the most common objections to the Bible in a 2-5
    minute format.

4   JD Greear, *The Biggest Questions I Get On Genesis 1 and 2*. https://jdgreear.
    com/blog/the-biggest-questions-i-get-on-genesis-1-and-2/.

5   Timothy Keller tweet: https://twitter.com/timkellernyc/status/63617661451
    1001600

6   Derek Rishmawy, *'Who Are You Sleeping With?' My Conversation with Timothy
    Keller*, Patheos: Christ and Pop Culture, 12 Apr. 2013. Web. 06 Jan. 2017.

7   Ashley Null, *Thomas Cranmer's Doctrine of Repentance: Renewing the Power to
    Love*, Oxford: Oxford University Press, 2000.

8   Masao Takahashi, *Mastering Judo*, "Human Kinetics." p. viii. (2005).

9   Timothy Keller, *Real Confidence and the Blazing Torch*, from the sermon series,
    The Gospel According to Abraham. May 6, 2001.

10 Ibid.

11   Ibid.

12   Ibid.

13   Ibid.

14   Ibid.

15   Ibid.

16   Ibid.

17   MailOnline, Victoria Woollaston, "*How Often Do You Check Your Phone?*" *Daily Mail Online*, Associated Newspapers, 29 Oct. 2015. Web. 16 Feb. 2017. http://www.dailymail.co.uk/sciencetech/article-3294994/How-check-phone-Average-user-picks-device-85-times-DAY-twice-realise.html.

18   Quote by Dr. John Hammett, faculty at Southeastern Baptist Theological Seminary. Quote given in a Theology Hybrid weekend seminar, spring 2016.

19   Timothy Keller, *The Prodigal God* (Penguin Group, 2008), chapter 7, iBook page 101.

20   C. S. Lewis, *The Four Loves* (Harcourt, 1960), pp. 61-62.

21   Timothy Keller, *The Prodigal God* (Penguin Group, 2008), chapter 7, iBook page 102.

22   Timothy Keller, *Real Riches and the Ambitious Man*, Sermon Series: The Gospel According to Abraham. 29 April 2001.

23   Disclaimer: While this is a statement consistent with what we know of Liddell historically, there is, quite surprisingly, no factual evidence that he actually said it.